Start Your

HEALTH CARE

Career

Other Entrepreneur Pocket Guides include

Start Your Real Estate Career

Start Your Restaurant Career

Entrepreneur
MAGAZINE'S
POCKET GUIDES

Start Your
HEALTH CARE
Career

Entrepreneur Press and
Cheryl Kimball

Ep
Entrepreneur
Press

Editorial Director: Jere L. Calmes
Advisory Editor: Jack Savage
Cover Design: Beth Hansen-Winter
Production and Composition: Eliot House Productions

This publication is designed to provide accurate and authoritative information in regard to the subject matter covered. It is sold with the understanding that the publisher is not engaged in rendering legal, accounting or
other professional services. If legal advice or other expert assistance is
required, the services of a competent professional person should be sought.

Library of Congress Cataloging-in-Publication Data

ISBN-13: 978-1-59918-026-7 (alk. paper)
ISBN-10: 1-59918-026-X (alk. paper)

Printed in Canada
12 11 10 09 08 07   10 9 8 7 6 5 4 3 2 1

Contents

Chapter 5

Nursing 59

Chapter 6

Specialized and Higher-Level Work in Health Care 73

Chapter 7

The Working Environment 91

Chapter 8

Building a Resume 103

Chapter 9

Getting Hired and Getting Ahead 117

Chapter 10

On Your Own 133

Resources 145

Glossary 147

Index 151

Acknowledgments

Thankfully, there are millions of caring individuals who have chosen to dedicate themselves to taking care of the rest of us. They are an admirable bunch, and I feel privileged to have interviewed a small number of them for this book.

Thanks go to those people who agreed to be interviewed for the profiles at the beginning of each chapter. Everyone I asked enthusiastically let me steal some of their valuable time to talk about their careers. Each and every one fascinated me with their dedication, their unique career paths, and the seriousness with which they take on their role of caring for others.

Thanks to all of my friends and family who seem to have become accustomed to my queries for help each time I am writing a new book. They always come through with great responses to my e-mails and phone calls asking things like, "Do you have any friends or friends of friends in health care that might let me interview them for a book I'm writing?"

Thanks to one of my favorite people, Jere Calmes, publishing director at Entrepreneur Press. Jere is a kind, caring, and patient man. Karen Thomas, Entrepreneur assistant editor, sends me supportive e-mails that I appreciate. And Karen Billipp, who does production and composition for Entrepreneur books, is a great professional and a good friend as well.

Thanks to my immediate family, especially my husband Jack Savage, who has heard many health care stories, and my mother, Joyce Kimball, who must be tired of hearing the constant refrain about how busy I am.

And thanks too go to the current dogs in my life, Dot, Dash, Pellie, and Tex, who keep me company laying all around my desk while I am working, sometimes not-so-patiently wondering when this project will be done and they will get a walk in the woods. Right now, you guys. Let's go.

Preface

Choosing a career in health care is something you should do with great forethought. You will probably need to spend time and money on education before making any money. You will probably work long hours. And sometimes the level of stress in such an intense industry as health care takes people by surprise. But if you go into it with your eyes wide open, a career in health care provides some of the most rewarding work life you can imagine.

Is Health Care Right for You?

Probably. Some specific jobs in the field may not suit your personality. If you really get queasy about blood and gore, you want to stay away from becoming an emergency room nurse, or perhaps from nursing all together. If you hate the thought of being trapped in one room most of the day, you would do best to avoid becoming a radiologist. If you don't like to work independently most of the time with little contact with colleagues, you wouldn't do well as a visiting home care nurse.

But the health care industry is so diverse that there really is something for everyone. You can work with the public, or not. You can work with just children, just the elderly, just men, just women, or a mix of all types of people. There's traditional paperwork or modern technology. The choice is yours. But you first need to understand your own personality. This book will help you do that in the context of considering working in health care.

Your Personal Goals

The health care industry isn't ripe for start-up businesses, but it is possible. Check Chapter 10 for help thinking through that angle of the industry. If you have a good imagination and can be flexible, there are opportunities for self-employment and entrepreneurship.

If your goal is to make a decent living, have some benefits, and contribute to the well-being of society, getting into health care is a great option. You can help people feel better, get better, or, as you shall learn, help them and their families have a peaceful and dignified end-of-life experience.

Set your goals in manageable increments. Decide on the specific health care career you want—there's one goal. Then find a school or college that will help you get there. There's another goal. Get through the program—there's a big goal accomplished. Find an environment you wish to work in—hospital, small clinic, emergency room, home care—another goal down. Then accomplish the goal of finding a job in that environment. After that, your main goal might be just to have a rewarding work life. Or maybe you will decide after a couple of years on the job that you would like to specialize more. Go for it!

Meaningful Work

Health care encompasses some of the most meaningful work out there. You help people with an unavoidable necessity—maintaining good health or solving a health problem. But you will also need, as in any other job, to pay attention to staying motivated in your work and avoiding burnout.

Motivation can come in many forms—finding a mentor you want to work with, going to a larger hospital, or from a rural hospital to an urban hospital, or vice versa. Traveling and working overseas can be motivating and reinvigorate your love of your field. Specializing in something general like pediatrics or something more specific like caring for premature babies can do the trick. Constantly look for the meaning in your work and the motivation that keeps it meaningful—that probably won't be too hard to do in a helping profession like health care.

CHAPTER 1

About the
Health Care Industry

PROFILE
Judy Savage
Registered Nurse

Getting her degree as a registered nurse (RN) was a midlife decision for Judy Savage. She started her schooling taking one course a semester while continuing her busy life as a homemaker and mother of three.

"While no mentor comes to mind," Judy says about her decision to go into nursing, "nurturing and caretaking certainly played into it." Judy feels these are personality traits that go hand-in-hand with nursing.

Before she ever began formal schooling, Judy had done a variety of nursing-related volunteer work. As a member of an organization whose focus was volunteerism, she worked in an orphanage, a long-term convalescent home for physically and mentally handicapped children, a mental hospital, and a nursery school for retarded children.

These volunteer experiences made Judy realize she should get some training, both to know more, to do more, and to be able to make some money at it. Judy got her two-year degree from a junior college associated with the University of Cincinnati. While in school, her clinical rotation gave her experiences in other kinds of nursing care, from ob/gyn to a nursing home. "I loved the geriatrics," she says. "But my mom was elderly and needing a lot of care, and it just seemed too close." Judy landed on pediatrics as her area of concentration.

Today Judy is an RN in the pediatric hospice division of Cincinnati Children's Hospital. She often picks up her assignments for the day from her laptop computer. (Computers are a vital part of her work life, a change that has occurred just over the past decade.) Her day consists of traveling around the greater Cincinnati area. Children's Hospital's range includes southeastern Indiana and northern Kentucky, as well as Ohio, requiring her to be licensed in all three states.

Hospice care also requires her to be on call. "Different people take to being on call differently," she says. "It can be more confining." Whether a nurse needs to be on call varies by the type of job. Although she finds it stressful to be responsible for all those patients, Judy knows it simply goes with the territory.

Home care, keeping people out of the hospital, is a major trend in nursing care. Judy has seen it grow steadily in the 15 years she's been in it.

In pediatric hospice, Judy faces the terminal illnesses of young patients daily. How does she deal with that? "In my years volunteering on lifesquad, we would do advanced lifesquad on full arrest patients. It's invasive; it's not pretty. I was involved with a 'full code' on quite a few elderly patients. It became very clear to me that there should be death with dignity."

And then she gets such grateful comments from people. "The mother of a 13-year-old boy who recently died of leukemia told me how much she appreciated that her son never had to be in the hospital."

She adds, "I often have good memories of these kids; there's a good feeling in helping people die with dignity. The heroes aren't us, they are the caregivers in the home. I get to go home to my own bed at night. They are dealing with it day in and day out."

Judy has also taken her degree and experience and used it in varied situations, such as volunteering at an orphanage for AIDS-afflicted babies in Africa. Her hospital sent teams to the area affected by Hurricane Katrina and a friend has been to Belize.

Judy's advice to students just starting their nursing training is to get as much advanced training as they can. "If I were 20 years younger," she says, "I would go on to get my bachelor of science in nursing." Nursing has become so technical, she says, and there have been a lot of layers placed between the nurse and the doctor.

■   ■   ■

The health care industry of less than a 100 years ago is almost unrecognizable compared to the industry today. In the 1920s, my grandmother delivered her first two children at home with the assistance of her family doctor who arrived by horse and buggy. Grandpa retired to the garage, smoked cigars, and tinkered at the workbench until Doc Taylor came out and delivered the news that the healthy baby was crying in his mother's arms. Judy Savage, now nearing retirement, could not have imagined early in her career that she would, as a home care nurse, be connected to her office mostly via laptop computer.

Today, the majority of babies born to families in that same coastal fishing village are born at one of several very high-tech hospitals within a 40-mile range. Fathers are often present in the delivery room. And almost every possible piece of technology is within reach if something goes wrong. For those things not within reach, a helicopter can quickly deliver a patient to at least three large regional medical centers within a couple hours at most.

Times have changed—and for the good, if you are considering health care as a career choice. Even rural areas have substantial medical options, which has made health care a career path with lots of opportunity for anyone who's interested.

How It Got This Way

Health care has been subject to the chicken-and-the-egg syndrome. Health insurance (a concept that originated as early as the 1600s) has had an enormous impact on how health care is delivered. And the increase in the capabilities of health care have precipitated changes in the health insurance that pays for it.

One of the significant changes brought about by the increased control of health insurance is the fundamental way hospitals operate. Anyone who has been admitted to the hospital in recent years for any type of care, routine or emergency, has seen firsthand the desire of hospitals to discharge you as soon as possible. Part of that has been the result of research showing that for many conditions, the quicker you go back to normal life, the quicker and better you recover.

This has been especially evident in the world of childbirth—what several decades ago would have consisted of a multiday stay for routine births now involves only a couple of days.

Ongoing Trends

According to the American Nursing Association, nurses are the largest group of health care workers in this country. There are 2.9 million, and still there is a predicted shortage of close to 800,000 nurses by the year 2020. Nursing is certainly one of the few modern professions with job security.

Getting patients out of the hospital faster does not mean the need for fewer nurses. It's all about turnover—typically, there's someone to take a patient's place as soon as he or she leaves the hospital bed.

So the nursing profession has not been harmed by the decrease in hospital stays. In fact, nurses are in even higher demand, in part because there is a greater need for outpatient care.

As the medical industry gets more and more specialized, and more and more sophisticated with healing capabilities beyond imagination, the opportunities in health care support become greater as well. Specialized doctors need specialized assistants, and areas of specialization such as radiology, physical therapy, and anesthesiology also offer great potential for those with an interest in the health care field.

Statistics

Of the 20 fastest growing occupations, the U.S. Department of Labor's Bureau of Labor Statistics predicts eight to be in health care. More of the new jobs—estimated at 3.6 million—created between 2004 and 2014 will be in the health care industry than any other industry. And those jobs are probably going to be in the 545,000 establishments housing medical professionals.

Health care facilities are broken down by the U.S. Department of Labor into the following nine segments:

1. Hospitals
2. Nursing and residential care facilities
3. Physicians' offices
4. Dentists' offices
5. Home health care services
6. Offices of other health care practitioners, such as chiropractors, physical therapists, and psychologists
7. Outpatient care centers
8. Ambulatory health care services such as organ transport, blood banks, and ambulance and helicopter services
9. Medical and diagnostic labs

Industry Breakdown

The main category of health care that most people are familiar with is the medical doctor. Because of the intense and lengthy amount of education required to become a medical doctor, we are not including them in this book. But even so, that leaves a wide open field of possibilities.

Nurses

The nursing profession is by far the largest and most diverse of the health care related job market. Nurses at all levels are needed in all phases of health care, from doctor's offices to hospitals to the home care setting and everywhere in between.

Nurses can be general in their practice—the licensed practicing nurse (LPN), the registered nurse (RN), or nurse practitioner. Or they can be specialized—pediatrics, geriatrics, oncology nurses, you name it.

And where you want to land will have a great bearing on how much schooling you will need. The nursing profession starts at two-year degrees and goes to four-year degrees and beyond.

Nursing is so diverse and such a large part of the medical profession that all of Chapter 5 is devoted to it.

Assistants

The medical assistant is a critical part of the smooth flow of any medical office. The office assistant makes sure the office works as well as possible, runs the medical scheduling and billing software, and keeps records up to date and filed.

A general medical assistant may keep medical supplies filled, rooms cleaned after each patient, and perform as a "gopher" for doctors and nurses—it depends on the office and the number of other staff. Some offices have separate scheduling and accounting assistants; some offices are small and nurses do all of the medical supply refilling.

Working as a medical assistant is a great way to dip your toe into the medical world and see if the water feels soothing or turns you cold. You can see all factions of the particular environment you entered (doctor's office, hospital, emergency room) and see where—and if—you might want to get further education and head in a certain direction with your health care career.

Specialization

The medical world offers all kinds of possibilities for specialization. Radiology (x-rays), oncology (cancer), anesthesiology (making people unconscious), phlembotomy (taking blood), and lab work are just a few examples of areas in which you can specialize.

And you can specialize within those specialities. The radiologist can become expert in mammograms or bone x-rays. The oncology nurse can become a specialist in one kind of cancer or in one area of cancer treatment, like administering chemotherapy.

Dietitians represent a huge area of specialization—and from there more specialization can take place, such as diabetes or cancer nutrition.

Dentistry is another area of specialization within the medical world. And dental hygienists are in great demand as dentists' offices become larger and busier.

Adjunct Medical Careers

You may already have a degree in something else and wish to enter the medical profession. Like most industries, the medical world needs lots of adjunct professionals—people who are not medical professionals per se but who use their professions to specialize in the medical industry. Accountants and computer software engineers are just a couple possibilities. You can even be a salesperson, working for drug companies or medical equipment suppliers.

Urban, Suburban, or Rural?

Luckily, you can be in the medical field and work in almost any environment. Many urban areas of the country—Boston, for instance—are major medical hubs. Suburban or small metro areas—like Rochester, Minnesota, where the Mayo Clinic is located—also can have their fingers on the medical industry pulse. And don't discount rural America—some of the best hospitals in the world are located in rural towns. They may not house the latest in computerized technology and all the whiz-bangs of the urban or university-connected hospitals, but they often are within easy reach of those services and have had to step up to the plate in other areas to remain competitive.

Where there is a major hospital—either urban, suburban, or rural—there is also a wealth of adjunct medical offices such as GPs, physical therapists, or pain management clinics.

Who Is Suited for the Medical Industry?

The short answer is "almost anyone." The medical industry is so diverse that just about any personality type can find a home. The key is to make sure you find the home in the type of environment you want to be in. If people in distress make you stressed, if the sight of blood makes you queasy, and you don't do well in fast-paced environments, stay away from the emergency room.

But in a field where you can work with computers or people, be on the road or be in an office, or spend the day on the phone or talking one-on-one with patients in the treatment room, there really is a place for everyone. You then need to consider what kind of money you want/need to make and what kind of hours you like to keep.

The Bottom Line

What kind of money can you make in the medical field? As with most fields, that depends.

First, it depends on what kind of position you wish to have. If you are willing to devote yourself to your career, becoming specialized in a certain area either through work experience or through schooling, you will be able to get to the upper levels of the profession. Will you make $150 per hour? Probably not. But your weekly pay can get pretty high if you have the free time to put in lots of overtime nights and weekends being on call, working third shift, or doing weekends and holidays. As with anything, to make a lot of money you have to sacrifice time and money somewhere to get there.

Hospital workers, according to data from the U.S. Department of Labor's Bureau of Labor Statistics, make the most per hour of the health care industry workers. In 2004, those hourly wages for nonsupervisory positions exceeded an

TRENDS

The home care trend continues to explode. Elderly care is another area that, with the first baby boomers turning 65, will be a booming (sorry) business in the very near future.

average of $20.31. Registered nurses in the hospital environment were making an average of $25.66 per hour.

The other part of the bottom line is benefits. Most full-time health care jobs offer excellent benefits, but ironically, being in the medical profession does not mean you automatically get health insurance with your job. Private practices are not much different from any other small business—struggling to pay office leases and high insurance costs makes it difficult when it comes to offering employee health benefits.

The Crystal Ball

How bright is the future of the medical industry as a professional choice? Pretty bright. Health care in the United States is not going anywhere. We are one of the most progressive nations in the world when it comes to health care. (Health insurance is another story, but a high level of care is there if you can afford it.) That is unlikely to change.

About
You

PROFILE

Kathy Mains

Certified Medical Assistant

Nursing school was too demanding for her lifestyle at the time Kathy Mains entered the health care field, but she fully intended to go back once she was in a better position to commit to full-time schooling. In the meantime, she took a job as a nurse's aide in home care. And Kathy ended up liking her work so much she stayed with home care for almost ten years, and even won a CNA of the year award!

When her own health began to impact how much she was able to do the heavy lifting often required in home care, Kathy began to think of where she might take her health care career next. She had decided she didn't really want the responsibilities of a nurse and so gave up her original idea of nursing school. But she definitely wanted to stay in the medical field. A nurse she worked with suggested she check into becoming a medical assistant.

One of the community colleges in her area offered a two-year associate's degree program to become a National Certified Medical Assistant. Kathy graduated from that program and has spent the past two years as a floater with Wentworth-Douglass Physician's Services in Dover, New Hampshire.

A floater works for the hospital's network of primary care providers filling in wherever someone is needed. Kathy picks up her schedule via e-mail and knows about a month in advance what her schedule will be. It has been a big transition from home care, but she enjoys the variety of her work.

"No two offices are alike," Kathy says. "Everyone does things a little differently. You need to keep track of all the different offices' procedures and different types of tests."

Working as a floater allows Kathy to see a wide range of offices and meet many people. With this comes lots of opportunities to find out about job openings if a floater were to decide to settle full time in one office.

Kathy's day as a medical assistant typically runs 8:30 A.M. to 5 P.M. She serves as the front line for the providers with whom she works, taking signs and symptoms over the phone and consulting with the provider to see if the patient needs to come to the office, go to the emergency room, or see some other specialty provider.

However, her days are sometimes longer because the hospital has requirements for ongoing training. To remain licensed, medical assistants need to earn annual continuing education units (CEUs). Within the hospital, Kathy says, there are a lot of rules, regulations, policies, and procedures to keep up with and on-the-job training takes care of that.

Overall, Kathy finds her job as a medical assistant very rewarding. She gets good benefits. And these days she isn't really thinking about going on to specialize further because she is already doing what she enjoys most—helping people take care of their health.

■ ■ ■

Many people fall into the trap of concentrating on a certain career path because it offers the salary they think they should earn or it seems like an interesting profession.

They get their education, they find a good job, and after a year or two honeymoon learning the ropes, they begin to wonder if being locked in an office all day every day is the picture of what the rest of their life is going to look like.

The good thing about the medical field is that the possibilities of what you can choose for a career are so diverse that it can fit just about any personality. Kathy Mains, for example, chose family over the all-consuming pursuit of a nursing degree and the responsibility of a nursing career. Nevertheless, she has been able to have a rewarding career in health care, adjusting her work situation to suit her lifestyle. But you have to make sure you choose the right part of the industry to make that fit.

Your Best Day

One of the most important questions you should ask yourself about a career is, "How do I like to spend my day?" If you are 19 years old and think partying all night, sleeping until noon, and drifting into work for a couple hours before doing it all over again sounds appealing—well, like most 19 year olds, you need to get that out of your system first.

But seriously, no matter what your age, thinking realistically about what comprises an interesting day to you is critical. Is it important for you to be outside, no matter what the season, no matter what the temperature, no matter what the weather? Or do you need to be in a comfortable indoor environment where the temperature is always the same, winter or summer, and you have easy access to clean bathrooms, a coffee machine, and a few good lunch spots? Does the idea of sitting behind a desk for eight hours seem like a fate worse than death?

Besides the environmental aspect of your day, what do you envision yourself doing all day? Sitting in front of a computer? Talking on the phone? Interacting with colleagues? Interacting with clients?

What you decide you want to do should have some relation to your favored type of environment.

Your Personality

How you like to spend your day will be impacted greatly by your personality. If you are a gregarious type, you won't thrive in a career path that means you will be locked in a lab with nothing but a microscope for company the better part of the day. But if the idea of office politics makes your skin crawl, that microscope may be the best pal you ever had. Think about your personality in regard to your work life:

- *Your energy level.* Are you going a mile a minute most of the time and like it that way? Do you like to keep in shape and exercise regularly? You may thrive in a fast-paced environment like an emergency room or as an EMT or on the rescue squad of a fire department. Not only do those kinds of jobs require you to be on the go, but they also require that you be physically fit.
- *People person.* Are you one of those people always referred to as a "people person"? The kind who, if you

find yourself home alone, is always reaching for the phone to chat with someone? Like any industry, the medical field requires customer service people. And anyone in any field who interacts with a customer/client base is doing customer service. If you enjoy dealing with people and find that you have a knack for defusing difficult situations, you know how to make people feel comfortable, and you have the ability to explain complex issues in a simple way, the medical field has lots of places for you.

- *Perennial student.* Are you always taking classes in something or taking up a new hobby whether you teach it to yourself or take a workshop? If you love the learning environment, nursing can be extremely rewarding. To stay licensed, nurses are required to take a certain number of CEUs each year, depending on the state in which you work. And most parts of the medical profession include an element of surprise, when you never quite know what you will be dealing with next, and so the learning part comes in automatically.

- *Caretaking.* Finally, if you are the kind of person who is always in the caretaking mode, the medical field can be perfect for you. Besides the most obvious role of nursing, even the medical office assistant does a fair amount of caretaking. You may be helping someone work through the ever-more-complex health insurance system. You might be the first person patients see when they come in, and you can be instrumental in helping a client feel more at ease. Dietitians specializing in diabetes care are always helping patients take better control of their condition. The medical field is a perfect arena for the perennial caretaker.

Natural Qualities and Existing Qualifications

Everyone brings certain qualities and qualifications to the work table, and they don't have to be "official" ones. You will definitely need to get a degree to be a nurse and specialized training to be a radiologist, but don't discount the skills you have already developed:

- *Multi-tasking.* Ever had a job waiting on tables? There's a multi-tasking talent-building job if there ever was one. "Give those people coffee, drop the check to the next table on the way by to the table in the corner to take their order, and on the way back to the kitchen check on that other table to see if everything's OK, and stop by the table at the window to tell them I will be right back to get their drink order." Whew. Don't discount these kinds of jobs as highly skill-building. And multi-tasking abilities will come in handy in most health care careers, from the busy medical office to the emergency room.
- *Caretaking.* Never been a nurse, you say? What about the times you have stayed up all night with your preschooler? Or the care you give to your aging parents? Or the time you stayed the week with your in-laws to

help while your mother-in-law got back on her feet after a nasty fall? Make a list of the times you have been a caretaker to others.

- *Accounting/bookkeeping.* Are you the family accountant? Do you keep meticulous track of your checking account? Have you worked in any jobs involving running a cash register? These involve math/accounting skills.

- *Computer work.* There is hardly a profession you can think of these days that doesn't involve computers on some level. The medical industry is no different. Front office people use computers for scheduling appointments, ordering supplies, looking up medical information, contacting health insurance companies, and contacting government agencies. X-rays are mostly computerized. Digital and electronic are the buzzwords for this fast-paced industry—any experience you have with computers is applicable. Even if you have not used any medical software programs, the fact that you know how to turn a computer on and use drop-down menus is skill enough for most programs to walk you through how to use them.

- *Customer service.* Any business of any kind in any industry relies on good customer service to help it stand out. As with any industry, there are many medical offices that clients can choose from to do business with. A friendly office with helpful staff is one key to clients choosing your office over another. If you have worked before, you have performed customer service. Knowing how to be supportive and informative without being condescending will enable you to provide excellent customer service to patients.

What Are Your Plans for Your Career?

Before you launch into any education to prepare yourself for a job in the health care field, you should decide whether you want a career or a job. If you are simply looking for a rewarding job, you can find that in the health care industry without having to spend a lot of time and money getting an education.

If you want health care to be your career and you want to specialize in a certain area of health care, education will be important. What you pursue for an education will depend on what you decide you are interested in. In many cases, a two-year degree will be sufficient. If you want to specialize (and make more money), you may need to stretch that two-year education into four years (or beyond).

Unless you are in a hurry and want to go get a two-year degree and get going on a health care career, don't discount the "on-the-job-training" method. You could start out with a front-desk job in a medical office while investigating which areas of the field you see as holding your interest. Interview your co-workers about their individual jobs. You may be pleasantly surprised to find that your employer offers education benefits—you may be able to work and go to school, have your schooling paid for, and find your new job in your chosen career without leaving your current company.

The Money Side

Money can be a motivating factor in career decisions, and careers in health care are no different. Just because you are doing "good work" helping people get well or maintain health does not mean you can't make a good living doing it.

Is money the main thing you are interested in when it comes to your work life? If so, you will definitely want to plan to get an education and specialize, which is the best way— short of spending years becoming a medical doctor—to make money in the health care field.

The other way to make a significant income is being a salesperson for medical supply houses or drug companies (the latter probably providing the better money). This can be a step removed from being in the midst of the helping profession, but it is still helping people maintain health—think of all the people who are taking medications that without them would lead much less comfortable lives.

Be realistic about your thoughts on money. And certainly don't be embarrassed about wanting to make a good living. We all need an income to maintain a lifestyle.

Leader or Follower?

How much money you make can also depend on whether you like to be a worker or a manager. Management has the potential to make more money than the "worker." Management will, however, tend to put you one step away from caregiving. Typically, at the management level your day-to-day work is with the staff, and that staff is providing the actual health care services.

That said, there is a lot of caretaking that takes place when it comes to managing people. And it is very rewarding to help staff members realize their own career goals.

Management positions usually don't materialize at the beginning of your career. You need to put in some years working in the field. But if management is in your sights, you will want to gear your early years toward that goal, getting experience in different aspects of the health care industry to give you a broad perspective of how things work to better manage an office or department.

Training, Education,
and Background

One day, while still in high school, Kelly Blake was sitting with her mom and some horseback riding friends talking about what she might do for a career. Her criteria was that she wanted something that would pay enough to do what she wanted to do, including having horses. One of the friends at the table suggested dental hygiene.

Kelly ended up in the Allied Health Program at the University of Vermont. (The program has since moved to the local tech college because of the cost of keeping the lab space and multi-thousand dollar dental chairs). She describes the college as strict—no skipping classes, someone would come get you—and says it seemed like family.

For the first year, she was in classes with many students from the nursing program. In anatomy class, they worked on human cadavers. The classes were big and included many labs; Kelly found that she really enjoyed the sciences.

They first practiced dental work on mannequins; then the students turned to each other. At the end of the first year, they started seeing actual patients.

The program is difficult to fit into two years, but Kelly was determined to do that. She took chemistry over the summer and crammed in her general education classes, graduating in 2003. She then took her New England Regional Boards. When asked if the tests were difficult she said, "I walked out not really knowing if I passed or not." She did. Then she took her Vermont State Boards, as well as a state jurisprudence test to check students' knowledge of the legal aspects of dental hygiene—what they can and cannot do, when the dentist has to be present, and other issues. She also took a New Hampshire jurisprudence test and became licensed in both states.

Kelly began her first job in July of 2003 in Vermont, and it was clear to her from the very beginning that this was a good place for her. "I really liked my colleagues. One of the dentists had been there for years and was real experienced; the other was just out of school and had learned things in the same way I had. The other hygienist was great; she had been there for 20 years. She knew everything, and was willing to show me everything."

Kelly stayed for two years and then decided to go on an extended cross-country trip with a couple of friends who had just graduated from college. She gave her workplace three months' notice. The dentists offered to let her come back, but Kelly had decided to move away and didn't take them up on their offer.

One of the reasons she decided to move was that she wanted to work in a less rural practice. Although she is always extremely grateful when patients come in and knows full well the financial burden of dental work, she was interested in working in a more affluent community closer to a strong employment base where people could afford regular dental care and were more likely to have employee dental benefits.

Kelly had considered going on in school to become a dentist but changed her mind. "I know I would like the work itself," she says, but she ultimately decided that the added stress and reduced flexibility didn't appeal to her. Now Kelly is thinking more about getting a bachelor's degree, maybe in public health, which would open up the possibility of teaching in a hygienist program.

Kelly has a little advice for those considering dental hygiene work. First, you really have to like it. "If you think to yourself 'I can't imagine looking in someone else's mouth all day,' don't do it. You need to think about it as just your job, and you do it."

Also, Kelly recalls that she hated her clinical experience while in school. "Don't worry," she advises, "being in the field on the job is much better than being a student."

Lastly, she advises, "Don't work for a dentist you don't like or whose methods you disagree with. Dentists are different, and your work life will be much more enjoyable if you and the dentist see eye to eye about dental care."

■   ■   ■

As the health care industry becomes more complex, more and more education is required for jobs in the field. Many community colleges are stepping up to fill the need for training and advanced education.

While it is possible to do some level of nursing without a formal degree, to be a nurse or almost any other medical specialist, you want to plan to get an education. Not only will you want to start out on the path to job searching with a degree in hand, but also for careers like nursing and—as we saw with Kelly Blake—dental hygiene, you are also expected to pass a national exam and get licensed according to state regulations. And after all of that, many health-related professions are required to take ongoing continuing education throughout their careers to maintain their licenses.

By Degrees

Although you need to plan to obtain some kind of advanced degree to have a career in the medical industry, as with everything, there are exceptions. Opportunities do exist to get on-the-job training and experience that is sufficient to allow you to expand your job responsibilities. But much of the medical world is technical by nature and regulated by state and federal agencies that require staff to have completed a certain number of hours in accredited school programs and perhaps even to have passed state or federal licensing exams. If you want a solid career in health care, you will want to plan some schoolwork into your career track.

The sheer number of settings that require nursing staff—hospitals, medical offices, retirement homes, rehabilitation institutions, schools—means the number of nurses needed to support quality medical care is huge. Because nursing represents the majority of positions in the medical-industry career track, I'll start there. What kind of degree does it take to become a nurse?

Licensed Practical Nurse (LPN)

The licensed practical nurse (called licensed vocational nurses in Texas and California) typically requires one year of education at one of the approximately 1,200 state-approved programs in the United States. All states and the District of Columbia require the passing of the licensing exam, NCLEX-PN (National Council Licensure Examination for Licensed Practical/Vocational Nurses), after finishing a state-approved practical nursing program. These programs are available at vocational/technical schools, community/junior colleges, as well as some high schools, hospitals, and colleges and universities.

The one-year program covers classroom work in nursing concepts, patient care, anatomy/physiology, medical-surgical nursing, pediatrics, obstetrics, psychiatric nursing, drugs, nutrition, and first aid. The program also includes supervised clinical practice, usually in a hospital setting.

The NCLEX-PN exam is developed and administered by the National Council of State Boards of Nursing (NCBN). It covers four categories, including safe and effective care environment, health promotion and maintenance, psychological integrity, and physiological integrity.

NCBN sponsors sessions where students can learn more about the NCLEX tests and computer adaptive testing in general. The NCLEX-PN test time allotment is five hours, and the test contains between 85 and 205 items.

Once licensed as an LPN/LVN, students can advance their training with an LPN-to-RN program.

Registered Nurse (RN)

The road to being a registered nurse is, not surprisingly, lengthier and more complex than that of becoming an LPN. You can become an RN with a two-year degree, but many people opt for a four-year bachelor of science in nursing (BSN) program in order to broaden their scope and earn a higher salary. A four-year program can lead to administrative positions and is required before moving on to a master's or other graduate nursing program. Graduate level work can lead to consulting, teaching, and research positions.

Hundreds of programs offer bachelor's degrees in nursing. There are also accelerated programs for those who already hold a bachelor's degree in another field. During the four-year degree, students can choose to specialize in numerous RN-based positions from midwifery to anesthesiology.

TIP

RNs fill management positions in hospitals, emergency rooms, home-based care, and other health care business-oriented positions.

The RN candidate is required to take the NCLEX-RN exam, which is allotted six hours for testing and includes 75 to 265 items. RNs are licensed by the state, and some states have reciprocal agreements whereby the RN can be licensed in one or more states without recertification in other states.

Other Education

Most non-nursing health care positions require other kinds of education, often in the form of one- or two-year associate's degree programs. Some, such as Emergency Medical Technicians, require specialized training. Although for some positions, graduating from specialized programs is not required, a degree does give you a jump start in getting a job at a higher entry level than you would without a degree.

An MBA could be a very useful degree in the medical world. An MBA combined with a medical-specific associate's degree could get you into a management position where you could make substantially more income.

Perhaps you are a teacher looking to change professions—there are lots of teaching opportunities in the medical world, from patient education to teaching at the community college or university level, or teaching programs such as EMT classes.

Look deeply at your own background and consider the possibilities of where your education and background could fit into the health care world.

On-the-Job Training

Even with a one- or two-year degree in hand, you will find on-the-job training is a key aspect to getting ahead in the health care field. Most education programs require that you work in the field before you graduate. This is where you will get a full appreciation for how important it is to get in there and get your hands dirty with whatever field you have decided upon. There's just nothing like real-life experience, whether it's changing a bandage, drawing blood, being amidst the controlled (eventually!) chaos of an accident scene, or trying to transcribe real-world medical records. It just isn't the same without the urgency of real patients behind what you are doing.

Volunteer Work

Volunteer work is covered in more detail in Chapter 8, which will help you build your health care resume. Don't underestimate volunteer work for great hands-on experience that you can draw on when you begin work in health care.

Keep track of any volunteer or in-the-field work that you do. Sometimes this can be transferred into credit in an associate's degree program.

Other Related Work Experience

There are many things you can do, or may have already done, in your work life that can be useful in your medical career.

Your duties in a medical office may entail some level of finance work, from daily bookkeeping to monthly accounting. Perhaps you ran your own business and took a finance course to learn how to keep the books—that experience may come in handy in your health care work as well.

Management jobs that you have had can be great experience for managing a medical office. Having the experience of employees reporting to you is a skill that can be utilized in almost any field—people are people no matter what kind of work they are doing. People management skills are very valuable. In professions like nursing, EMT work, or social work, where the burn-out factor can be very high, a person with proof that he or she can keep workers happy and productive is a skill worth flaunting.

Qualities for Success

A health care worker in almost any aspect of the medical field can benefit from certain personal qualities. Chaos isn't the perogative of the emergency room alone. Most medical offices experience chaotic times where the waiting room is overfilling with patients, the schedule is backed up, and the doctor gets called off for an emergency. Here are some skills you might want to brush up on.

People Skills

Although you probably won't find a class called "people skills," many skills-based classes relate to people skills.

Consider taking a communications class or join a group like Toastmasters where you can learn to be comfortable with public speaking. Most times, people just want to know the problem. If you have impatient clients in the waiting room, you can defuse tension by simply explaining the situation. You don't have to reveal information about a patient or anything but also don't give some lame excuse. Maybe you can do something innovative like make an arrangement with a local food establishment to deliver snacks or coffee or haul out a couple board games. Don't be afraid to try something different (with permission of the practice provider of course).

Listening

Find a workshop that teaches better listening skills. These kinds of less-concrete skills are often taught through career seminars. Many times we get into conflicts with people simply because we heard something different from what they were telling us. Sometimes it is lack of ability to communicate on the patient's part. But the onus is on the health care worker to understand where the patient is coming from.

Patience

This probably should come first, but all of these traits are of primary importance: If you don't have people skills or communication skills or patience, but you still want to work in health care, you should be sure to find a behind-the-scenes job like working in a lab or doing other diagnostic work. Working one-on-one with a patient when taking x-rays requires a different set of skills than trying to handle a waiting room full of patients whose appointments are all behind schedule.

Those people who have raised children probably have more of a handle on the patience skill. Also, being familiar with your job and knowing what to tell people can help you be more patient.

Self-Confidence

Learning medical procedures and being able to explain medical information to patients in a language they can understand requires a certain amount of self-confidence. If you don't feel as if you are starting out with a lot of self-confidence when it comes to health care, be assured that that will improve with time on the job. But diving in and getting that on-the-job experience will require you to muster up all the self-confidence you can. Patients pick up on lack of confidence, especially children. This can translate into concern about your ability and can make procedures more difficult. Think about your confidence level in those things you know well. And just keep trying and know that it will come in time.

What Does It Take to Advance?

You have your certification or license or undergraduate degree for the area of health care you have chosen. You've got your entry-level job. What now?

Work Hard!

Get to work on time. Early in fact. Try not to take sick days for the first six months and definitely don't take vacation time in that period unless you forewarned your employer before you were hired about plans you already had made.

Don't have your hand on the handle to the exit door the second the clock's little hand hits the end of your designated shift—linger a few minutes, tidy up your desk or the waiting room, or whatever. Wear appropriate clothing. Don't get caught up in office politics (it will be inevitable, but at least wait a few months).

Be ready and willing to learn what you need to in order to help the office run smoothly. Be available for overtime if it is offered. In other words, work hard.

Don't Complain

Don't complain about having to be on call—or anything else for that matter. You are working in your chosen field, what is there to complain about? It is fairly certain that no one forced you to take the job. Even if you don't envision yourself in the job for the rest of your career, or even beyond a year, do the best you can until you find the next step for you.

Stay Awhile

When you take a job, plan to stay at least a year. First, it takes several months to get to know a place and feel like you might be able to enjoy it there. Give it time. Second, think of your resume. You don't want to list job after job with only a few months in each. Giving a job at least a year not only shows good faith, but also lets future employers know you actually stayed long enough to learn something that can benefit you in the job they have to offer.

Keep Your Ears Open

Always assume that your next job might be with the person standing in front of you—a drug sales rep, another doctor, a nurse from the hospital. These personal connections are the best way to get the next great job in your long and enjoyable health care career.

General Jobs in
Health Care

PROFILE
Steve Favreau
Chiropractor

Steve Favreau went to school to be a teacher and pursued a teaching career once he graduated from college. But a few years into teaching, he started thinking about a career change. When he went to a chiropractor because of a back injury, he had what he calls one of those "a-ha moments." He had been searching for a new career, and it felt good to have made a decision.

Steve had avoided science courses in his undergrad schooling, so he had to enroll in some pre-med classes in Boston before going to chiropractic school—and he discovered he loved the sciences. Once finished with those classes, he went to Iowa to attend the Palmer College of Chiropractic, a school begun in the late 1800s by the founder of chiropractics, Daniel David Palmer. This four-year program included the required internship, one of the main differences with an MD program where you are required to begin your residency after your medical schooling.

After passing the national boards, Steve got a job in a chiropractic office in Lawrence, Massachusetts. He learned a lot about the business side of things, and the next time the state boards came up, he became licensed in Massachusetts. Shortly afterwards, the chiropractor in the office in which he worked died.

Steve took over the practice, but it was a personal injury practice, a more fast-paced environment than the family practice environment he had in mind. He stayed there for two years. When he arrived home from an extended honeymoon in Europe, a friend called to tell him that there was a chiropractic practice for sale in New Hampshire. So Steve decided to buy it. The former owner of the practice stayed for three months and helped with the transition. Steve describes the situation as ideal. Rather than opening a brand new practice and needing to cover overhead while gaining clientele, he walked into a practice with an existing client load.

Those beginning years, though, were the golden years for chiropractics. The field was becoming more accepted by the public and by the insurance world as a valuable treatment option. But managed care began to change all that, dictating the fees that chiropractors could charge and restricting patients on their number of visits.

"The relationship between a health care provider and a patient is a sacred one. This [managed care] wasn't to improve health care, this was to make more money for the middle person," says Steve.

He ended up having to take on side jobs to make money, ironically consulting for the insurance industry. And even though it started to even out a little, almost 20 years after buying into his own practice, Steve began to be disillusioned with his chosen career. "It took the joy out of it. I didn't expect to be a millionaire, but I did expect to make a living as a professional."

Now Steve is headed into a new career; well, a new old career—he's going back to teaching. "After 20 years in practice and after turning 50, I reassessed where I was at. I've been frustrated with the nation's politics, and I tried to figure out how I could make some mark. I decided teaching was where I could have some impact."

Steve still plans to practice part time. "I like chiropractics. People come to you, they are in pain, and usually I can help them. I never dreaded going to work."

Steve has advice for those thinking about getting into a medical career: Spend at least six months to a year talking with practitioners of all kinds before deciding what field to get into. And take as little money out in school loans as possible—don't trap yourself with years and years of school loan payments. It's worth it, he thinks, to take an extra year to make money before going to school instead of having to take several years after to pay it off.

■ ■ ■

Because nursing is not only the largest segment of the health care industry but also has the second largest number of job opportunities overall, nursing is covered in Chapter 5. Even so, there are hundreds of ways besides nursing that you can pursue a rewarding health care career. Some of them are covered here and some in Chapter 6.

Dental Hygienist

Dental hygienists are usually the first people patients see in a dentist office after they get in the chair. Hygienists examine patients' teeth and gums, clean teeth, teach patients about good oral hygiene, and record their findings in patient charts, including the presence of diseases or abnormalities.

Hygienists are responsible for taking and developing dental x-rays. In some states, according to the U.S. Department of Labor's Bureau of Labor Statistics, hygienists are allowed to administer anesthetics; place and carve filling materials, temporary fillings, and periodontal dressings; remove sutures; and smooth and polish metal restorations. Although the dentist is the one to diagnose diseases, hygienists can prepare tests that the dentist interprets to diagnose diseases. And a hygienist usually works chairside with the dentist during treatment.

Dental hygienists are key in teaching patients how to maintain good oral health. For example, they discuss the importance of diet, teach about selecting toothbrushes, and actually show patients how to brush and floss their teeth.

The dental world has advanced considerably in the last decade. For one thing, it has become very computerized; in updated offices, dental hygienists have chairside computer terminals to track patients' dental charts, schedule new appointments, and keep track of other procedures and tests. And hygienists now routinely wear protective gloves, eyewear, and masks to prevent the spread of infectious diseases.

As for work hours, flexibility is the name of the game with dental hygienists. Dentists typically hire hygienists part time, usually two or three days per week. Most hygienists work for more than one dentist in order to fill out a five-day work week.

The average wage of dental hygienists in 2004 was about $28 per hour with wages varying by geographic location and size of practice. Health and vacation benefits are typically contingent on full-time employment, which covers less than half of all dental hygienists. However, good dental benefits are typical for full- and part-time hygienists. Schools and other institutions sometimes hire dental hygienists to work specifically for them.

To work as a dental hygienist, you must become licensed by the state in which you plan to practice. This entails graduating from an accredited dental hygiene school, usually with an associate's degree, and passing a written exam administered by the American Dental Association and a clinical exam administered by a state or regional testing agency.

Plan to take classes in anatomy and physiology, chemistry, pharmacology, microbiology, and other sciences as well as more hands-on dental-related classes. Personal traits should include manual dexterity and an ability to work well with the public and as a team member with colleagues.

The U.S. Bureau of Labor indicates that dental hygienists are a fast-growing job segment and expects it to remain that way in the future.

Medical Assistant

Medical assistants have a wide range of job descriptions, but 60 percent of medical assistants work in physicians' offices. This is another medical profession that has a rosy future. The U.S. Department of Labor predicts that the best outlook is for those who get formal training such as a one-year certification or two-year associate's degree, but you can become a medical assistant through on-the-job training.

The medical assistant's job is extremely varied and depends on the needs of a particular office, but in general, duties can range from administrative tasks such as record-keeping, filing, scheduling, answering the phone, and greeting patients to clinical duties that vary and often depend on state law. Clinical duties may include taking medical histories and recording vital signs, explaining treatment procedures to patients, preparing patients for examination, and even assisting the physician during the examination. Some medical assistants collect and prepare laboratory specimens or perform basic laboratory tests on the premises, dispose of contaminated supplies, sterilize medical instruments, and carry out other general clinical duties. They may also instruct patients about medications and special diets, prepare and administer medications as directed by a physician, authorize drug refills as directed, telephone prescriptions to a pharmacy, draw blood, prepare patients for x-rays, take electrocardiograms, remove sutures, and change dressings. Other duties depend on the specifics of the practice you work in.

You can also specialize as a medical assistant, working, for instance, with an eye doctor or foot doctor and performing duties specific to those specialties. These also may require passing special certification programs.

Hours for medical assistants are as varied as the types of work they do. Full-time, part-time, temporary, or permanent jobs are all available. Salaries average in the mid-20s. Work conditions, like most medical professions, are usually in clean, well-lit, comfortable offices. Besides physician's offices, medical assistants work in other medical arenas including hospitals, urgent care facilities, and specialty practices.

Medical assistants almost always work with the public, so you must be well-groomed and be able to communicate well, especially when explaining a physician's orders to patients. You must be able to be courteous in even the most trying situations. Some manual dexterity and visual acuity is needed, depending on the type of office you are in.

Personal and Home Health Aides

Home health care is on the rise, and personal and home health aides are helping make that happen. This is mostly a very entry-level position; it is not highly skilled, does not require any specific certification, and because of all that, is also lower on the pay scale than many health care jobs. Personal aides often work part time, so benefits are not available.

According to the Department of Labor, most personal aides work either with the disabled or the elderly, helping them with tasks from cooking meals to getting dressed. Aides usually have more than one client. These can be long-term positions or short-term aid provided to people who have been recently discharged from the hospital. They may help families with childcare issues when a parent has become temporarily or permanently disabled.

Home health aides do more health-related work, perhaps helping to plan meals for a person with a specific medical condition. They usually work under the supervision of a registered nurse, social worker, or other health care professional.

Home health aides need to be cheerful and flexible. They must be able to adapt to many different home settings. They need to be in good health and expect to work hard. They may need some health screenings and criminal record screening prior to being hired because they go into people's homes.

They are sometimes self-employed home care aides, but most work through a home care service where they are assigned clients and are supervised by medical staff. Being a home care worker of any kind is high on emotional demand. Average pay in 2004 was just over $8 an hour. Some are required to be on call some of the time. This and off-hours work can mean a bit higher wages.

Demand for this type of work is expected to increase dramatically in the next decade.

Pharmacy Aide/Pharmacy Technician

Pharmacy technicians help licensed pharmacists provide medication and other health care products to patients. Technicians usually perform routine tasks to help prepare prescribed medication for patients, such as counting tablets and labeling bottles. Technicians work under the supervision of the pharmacist and refer any questions regarding prescriptions, drug information, or health matters to the licensed pharmacist.

Pharmacy aides work closely with pharmacy technicians. They often are clerks or cashiers who primarily answer telephones, handle money, stock shelves, and perform other clerical duties. Pharmacy technicians usually perform more complex tasks than do pharmacy aides, although in some states the duties and job titles of the two positions may overlap.

Technicians may be on the receiving end of written prescriptions or requests for prescription refills from patients. They also may receive prescriptions sent electronically from doctors' offices. Technicians verify orders and prepare prescriptions, retrieving, counting, pouring, weighing, measuring, and sometimes actually mixing medications. They also create labels, select containers, and affix the prescription and auxiliary labels. Once a prescription is filled, technicians price and file the prescription. The prescription must be checked by a pharmacist before it is given to the patient. Technicians also do administrative work such as establishing and maintaining patient profiles, preparing insurance claim forms, and stocking and taking inventory of prescription and over-the-counter medications.

Pharmacy technicians also work in hospitals, nursing homes, and assisted-living facilities as well as in the retail and mail-order world. Here they have added responsibilities, including reading patients' charts and preparing and actually delivering the medicine to patients. Still, the pharmacist must check the order before it is delivered to the patient.

The work environment for the pharmacy technician and pharmacy aide tends to be clean, organized, well-lighted, and well-ventilated. Most of the workday, however, is spent on your feet. Technicians and aides may be required to lift heavy boxes or to use stepladders to retrieve supplies from high shelves.

Technicians work the same hours that pharmacists work. These may include evenings, nights, weekends, and holidays, particularly in facilities such as hospitals and many retail pharmacies that are open 24 hours a day.

Although most pharmacy technicians receive informal on-the-job training, employers, according to the U.S. Department of Labor, favor those who have completed formal training and certification. That said, there is currently little in the way of state and no federal requirements for formal training or certification of pharmacy technicians. Employers who have insufficient resources to give on-the-job training often seek formally educated pharmacy technicians. The military, some hospitals, proprietary schools, vocational or technical colleges, and community colleges offer formal education programs. Many training programs include internships in which students gain hands-on experience in pharmacies. Students receive a diploma, a certificate, or an associate's degree, depending on the program.

Prospective pharmacy technicians may gain an advantage by working as an aide first. Also, working in industries that require strong customer service and communication skills is helpful, as is experience managing inventories and using computers. Technicians entering the field need strong mathematics, spelling, and reading skills. A background in chemistry, English, and health education may also be beneficial. Some technicians are hired without formal training, but under the condition that they obtain certification within a specified period to retain their employment.

The Pharmacy Technician Certification Board administers the National Pharmacy Technician Certification Examination, a voluntary (in most states) exam. As this profession grows, more employers are expecting potential technicians to have become certified through this exam, which gives those who pass it the title of Certified Pharmacy Technician. Like most licensing exams, it is offered several times per year at various locations nationally, and recertification is required every two years.

Technicians must complete 20 contact hours of pharmacy-related topics within the two-year certification period to become eligible for recertification. Contact hours are awarded for on-the-job training, attending lectures, and college course-work. At least one contact hour must be in pharmacy law. Contact hours can be earned from several different sources, including pharmacy associations, pharmacy colleges, and pharmacy technician training programs. Up to ten contact hours can be earned when the technician is employed under the direct supervision and instruction of a pharmacist.

Successful pharmacy technicians must, above all, be attentive to detail and precise, because this can mean life or death in some situations and with some medications. They are also expected to be alert, observant, organized, dedicated, and responsible. They should be willing and able to take directions. Because they interact daily with patients, coworkers, and health care professionals, they need to be good communicators.

Seventy percent of pharmacy tech jobs were in retail pharmacies in 2004. The remaining 30 percent were mostly in hospitals with a smattering of jobs in mail order and internet pharmacies, wholesalers, or the federal government. Average salary was in the low $11 per hour range.

Aging baby boomers once again make this a burgeoning career path for the foreseeable future. Boomers are health conscious, eager to remain young and active, and willing to take medications to help them achieve that goal.

Physical Therapist (PT)

Yet another in a lineup of fast-growing health care careers, the physical therapist is in demand. Physical therapists help patients restore function, improve mobility, relieve pain, and prevent or limit temporary or permanent physical disabilities from injuries or disease. PT patients include accident victims as well as individuals with disabling conditions such as back pain, arthritis, heart disease, fractures, head injuries, and cerebral palsy. Physical therapists can also specialize or become proficient in areas like sports injuries or arthritis relief.

According to the DOL, another reason for the increased demand for physical therapists is that medical advances have allowed people to survive injuries that in the past resulted in death. Some of these severe injuries require physical therapy follow-up. The increased survival rate of infants with birth defects has also increased physical therapy needs.

Usually working in consultation with other medical professionals, physical therapists use therapies like electrical stimulation, hot packs and/or cold compresses, and ultrasound to relieve pain and reduce swelling. They may also use traction or deep-tissue massage to relieve pain. Therapists also teach patients to use devices such as crutches, prostheses, and wheelchairs. They also typically show patients exercises to do at home to enhance and expedite their recovery.

As their patient's therapy progresses, PTs often need to document progress by taking measurements of range of motion and comparing them to baseline measurements taken at the beginning of treatment. They then report these findings to the referral doctor.

Many physical therapists start their own practices with private clients and contract with doctor's offices and hospitals, but many also work out of hospitals, doctor's offices, and on the road in many different settings. Physical therapists need to be physically fit, and the job requires some heavy lifting and extended periods of time in stooping, kneeling, or crouching positions. You may also need to move heavy equipment like exercise machines, weights, and treatment tables, as well as help move patients in and out of wheelchairs and on and off treatment tables.

All 50 states require physical therapists to pass a licensing exam after finishing a four-year bachelor's degree from an accredited college or university program. PTs can also go for master's and doctorate degrees in almost half of the PT programs in the country.

The higher end of the PT salary scales nearly tips the $90,000 mark, with the average being around $60,000.

There has been some moderation of PT treatment with insurance restrictions on the number of visits allowed, but the overall increase in use of physical therapy should easily offset this.

Laboratory Technician

"Technician" and "technologist" are usually two different levels of the same position. A lab technician, for example, needs less schooling and has fewer responsibilities than a laboratory technologist. Technicians usually have a two-year associate's degree or certificate, and technologists usually have a four-year bachelor of science degree.

Laboratory tests are critical in helping detect, diagnose, and treat diseases. With preventive health care on the rise, tests are used to help with early detection of diseases or to find signs that disease could be imminent, as with tests for diabetes. Basically, lab tests look at cells and body fluids for bacteria, parasites, and other microorganisms.

Lab personnel often spend a lot of time looking into microscopes. They take fluids and tissue samples and make cultures, waiting to see if certain bacteria or viruses grow. Technicians may take samples, prepare samples, or run automated diagnostic equipment while lab technologists examine samples and diagnose presence of bacteria or other microorganisms.

There are some hazards associated with this type of work. The samples themselves may expose technicians to biological hazards and diseases while some of the reagents and other chemicals used may give off fumes. Depending on the type of work you do, there may be some stiffness from sitting in the same position while looking through microscopes. There is, however, enough variety in the job that you should seldom spend inordinate amounts of time in one position.

Many states require that lab personnel be licensed. Each state's department of health should be able to give you the information you need regarding licensing requirements.

Traits needed to be a competent laboratory worker include good analytical judgment and the ability to work under pressure. Results are often needed as quickly as possible to expedite the patient's road to recovery. Also, attention to detail is an important trait because there are many times when minor differences in test results—color changes, for example—can mean big differences in the diagnosis.

Surgical Technologist

What could be more exciting than being a member of the surgical operating team? That's what surgical technologists do. Exactly what they do depends on the setting, the type of surgery being done, and the number of other assisting personnel in the surgical suite during surgery.

Typically, before an operation gets underway, surgical technologists help prepare for surgery by setting up the operating room with the appropriate surgical instruments and equipment, sterile drapes, and sterile solutions. They assemble equipment, checking to ensure it is working properly and adjusting it where necessary. Technologists also get patients ready for surgery by washing, shaving, and disinfecting incision sites. They transport patients to the operating room, help position them on the operating table, and cover with sterile surgical "drapes" any areas outside the surgery site. Technologists also assist the surgical team with putting on sterile gowns and gloves and checking patients' vital signs during surgery.

Technologists may also help pass instruments to the surgeon, cut sutures where instructed, count sponges, needles, and other items to ensure they all are accounted for before the incision is stitched. And the technologist may be responsible for cleaning and restocking the surgical suite after an operation.

You probably need a strong stomach to be a surgical technologist. You are likely to be exposed to fluids, blood, and odors. Surgery requires standing on your feet for long periods of time and remaining alert throughout the surgery. You may also be exposed to communicable diseases.

Surgical assistants typically work a 40-hour week, but you most likely will be required to be on call on a rotating basis with other surgical personnel.

You will want to become certified, which means graduating from an accredited program and passing a national exam. You will need to renew your certification every five years.

The median income for a surgical technologist in 2004 was just over $34,000. You can significantly increase your salary by becoming a specialist, for instance, in open heart surgery or neurosurgery. Most surgical technologists work in the hospital setting.

Respiratory Care Practitioner

Respiratory care practitioners evaluate, treat, and care for patients with breathing or other cardiopulmonary disorders. They practice under the direction of a physician, assuming primary responsibility for all respiratory care therapeutic treatments and diagnostic procedures.

While the field is broken up into respiratory care therapists and respiratory care technicians, in clinical practice many of the daily duties of therapists and technicians overlap. Furthermore, the two have the same education and training requirements. However, therapists generally have greater responsibility than technicians. Respiratory therapists also are more likely to provide complex therapy requiring considerable independent judgment, such as caring for patients on life support in intensive-care units of hospitals.

Respiratory care practitioners evaluate and treat all types of patients, ranging from premature infants whose lungs are not fully developed to elderly people whose lungs are diseased.

They provide temporary relief to patients with chronic asthma or emphysema, as well as emergency care to those who are victims of a heart attack, stroke, drowning, or shock. The respiratory therapist's job may include other responsibilities such as smoking cessation counseling and diagnosis of sleep disorder respiratory problems. Treatments include administering oxygen or oxygen mixtures, chest physiotherapy, and aerosol medications.

According to the U.S. Department of Labor, the National Board for Respiratory Care (NBRC) offers certification and registration to graduates of programs accredited by the Commission on Accreditation of Allied Health Education Programs (CAAHEP) or the Committee on Accreditation for Respiratory Care (CoARC). Again, specializing in certain types of treatment or conditions and getting advanced education are the two ways of advancing in the respiratory care field.

As with all other health care careers that revolve around either infant care or elderly care, there should be no lack of jobs for the foreseeable future. Median salary for a respiratory therapists in 2004 was over $43,000.

Nursing

Her first job was in a neurosurgical unit in a large medical center. But when she spent time as a floater filling in wherever a short-staffed unit needed help, Kay loved it and decided she wanted to be a generalist. "I loved the diversity," she says.

Part of her floating involved emergency and intensive care, which led her to become certified in advanced cardiac life support (ACLS) in order to further increase her marketability. She worked at both the neurosurgical unit at a regional medical center outside Boston and at an inner city hospital in another Boston suburb as a floater, being paid per diem.

"I never had to worry about work," she says. "I was in demand because I was good at what I did. But you get burned out with the constant adrenaline rush. I had a chance to swing into long-term care as an educational nurse. I loved that, too."

This work was with a large distributive pharmacy for the long-term care industry. She moved within the company to become regional director of nursing, overseeing the nurse consultants in the company's sites all around New England. In this position, Kay also organized the disbursement of educational tools and arranged for educational seminars. But this role was eventually abolished, and Kay came again to acute care to her current position.

As case manager/clinical claims analyst, she makes sure the clinical pathways are being followed and the correct resources are being used. Thus, when insurance denies a claim, she can prove that a procedure was, in fact, medically necessary.

"I've been in nursing for 16 years," Kay says. "I love it. You can do anything, any shift, any capacity and make changes that fit your lifestyle. My job now allows me flexibility in my schedule and also to use my background cumulatively without the responsibility (or physical labor) of direct care and the management overload."

Unlike popular opinion, Kay thinks it is good that health care has evolved to such a consumer-driven market—she feels that this change compels individuals to become careful health care consumers and to become educated about their own health care.

■ ■ ■

The nursing component of the health care field is extensive enough to warrant a book all its own. Many positions in health care, such as some of those Kay Stevens filled, aren't traditional nursing positions but require or are enhanced by a nursing degree. And many specialty positions that don't involve direct patient care also require holders to be a registered or licensed practical nurse. Nursing is the foundation of health care.

According to the U.S. Department of Labor's Bureau of Labor Statistics, registered nurses comprise the largest component of the health care field, with about 2.4 million jobs. Studies have shown that patients thrive or not in direct correlation to the patient/nurse ratio at a medical facility.

Nursing Aide

Nursing aides—also known as nursing assistants, certified nursing assistants, geriatric aides, unlicensed assistive personnel, orderlies, or hospital attendants—perform routine tasks under the supervision of nursing and medical staff. These tasks include things like answering patients' call buttons, delivering messages, serving meals, making beds, and helping patients to eat, dress, and bathe. Aides also may provide skin care to patients; take their temperature, pulse rate, respiration rate, and blood pressure; and help them to get into and out of bed and walk. They may escort patients to operating and examining rooms, keep patients' rooms neat, set up equipment, store and move supplies, and assist with some procedures. Aides observe patients' physical, mental, and emotional conditions and report any changes to the nursing or medical staff. Nursing aides employed in nursing care facilities often are the principal caregivers, having far more contact with residents than do other members of the staff.

Licensed Practical Nurse (LPN)/Licensed Vocational Nurse (LVN)

The LPN or LVN is a main entry-level point of the nursing field. You don't have to become an LPN to be a registered nurse. And many LPNs decide to go on in their education and become RNs. But if you want a rewarding career in the medical field but don't have interest in advancing your career in a big way, the LPN may be perfect for you.

To become an LPN, you need to go through a state-approved one-year program and take the LPN licensing exam, the NCLEX-PN. LPNs typically work under the supervision of an RN.

Once licensed, their duties include basic bedside care, taking vital signs such as temperature, blood pressure, pulse, and respiration. They also prepare and give injections and enemas, monitor catheters, apply dressings, treat bedsores, and give alcohol rubs and massages. LPNs monitor their patients and report adverse reactions to medications or treatments. They collect samples for testing, perform routine laboratory tests, feed patients, and record food and fluid intake and output. To help keep patients comfortable, LPNs assist with bathing, dressing, and personal hygiene.

Laws vary from state to state as to what medications LPNs can administer and whether they are allowed to start the administration of intravenous fluids. Some LPNs help to deliver, care for, and feed infants. And with experience, an LPN degree may let you supervise nursing assistants and aides.

Beyond routine bedside care, LPNs in certain settings such as nursing care facilities help to evaluate residents' needs, develop care plans, and supervise the care provided by nursing aides. In doctors' offices and clinics, they also may make appointments, keep records, and perform other clerical duties. LPNs who do home care work may prepare meals and teach family members simple nursing tasks such as bandage changing and wound hygiene.

Registered Nurse (RN)

The registered nurse (RN), as the Department of Labor describes, is the foundation of health care. The Labor Department estimates that the nursing field will offer the second largest number of jobs of all occupations for the foreseeable future. This not only points to the huge number of environments in which the registered nurse works but also to the diversity of the specific work the RN performs.

Although many RNs specialize beyond general nursing or choose to work in a specific setting, they all perform, or start out by performing, basic nursing duties. These duties include treating patients, educating patients and the public about various medical conditions, and providing advice and emotional support to patients' family members. How much of each of these you perform as a nurse depends on the environment you work in and in the support resources that the facility has in place.

RNs also record patients' medical histories and symptoms, help to perform diagnostic tests and analyze results, operate medical machinery, administer treatment and medications, and help with patient follow-up and rehabilitation.

RNs teach patients and their families how to manage an illness or injury, including posttreatment home care needs, diet and exercise programs, and self-administration of medication and physical therapy. Some RNs are trained to provide grief counseling to family members of critically ill patients. RNs work to promote general health by educating the public on warning signs and symptoms of disease and where to go for help. RNs also might run general health screening or immunization clinics, blood drives, and public seminars on various conditions. And the registered nurse often supervises other health care workers in performing many of these tasks.

RN Specialization

As your career as an RN unfolds, you may find a specialty that appeals to you. There are four basic categories that nursing specialities fall under:

1. work setting or type of treatment, such as emergency room or chemotherapy;
2. disease, ailment, or condition, such as diabetes, arthritis, pregnancy, cancer, or HIV;
3. organ or body system type, such as cardiac, gastrointestinal, or dermatology; and
4. population, such as pediatrics, geriatrics, or low income.

Specialization can even go further. RNs may combine specialties from more than one area, for example, pediatric oncology or cardiac emergency. Some of this will come about from personal interests you develop as you become experienced in nursing, some of it is an offshoot of employer needs.

Following are some specializations common to registered nurses.

Ambulatory Care Nurse

Nurses in ambulatory care treat patients on an outpatient basis, usually in doctors' offices or health clinics. The range of illnesses and injuries is broad. In the electronic age, this kind of care also often encompasses what the Department of Labor refers to as *telehealth*—providing care and medical advice through electronic media such as teleconferencing or over the internet via web sites and chat rooms.

Critical Care

RNs involved in critical care are typically working in intensive care units in a hospital setting. They are often providing nursing to patients with cardiovascular, respiratory, or pulmonary problems that require round-the-clock care in a setting with significant medical monitoring and treatment equipment and resources.

Emergency

Emergency, or critical care, nurses care for patients with life-threatening medical conditions, often as a result of accidents or sudden conditions such as heart attack or stroke. Typically, this is in the emergency room setting where every hour brings a new experience to your career. Some emergency nurses choose to work in the lifesquad/ambulance setting, which brings you as close to fundamental medical care as you can get. And still others perform as flight nurses providing care to patients being flown by helicopter to other medical facilities.

Holistic

Holistic nurses usually combine traditional medicine with Eastern medicine such as acupuncture, massage, and aromatherapy, treating patients' mental health alongside their physical health in a "complementary medicine" fashion. This is becoming of more and more interest to the general population in the United States.

Home Health Care Nurses

Home care is one of the fastest growing segments of health care in this country. The home care nurse provides patient care in the home environment. Patients are often recovering from surgery, accidents, or childbirth.

Palliative Care/Hospice Nurse

Usually a segment of the home care nurse, hospice and palliative care nurses ease the pain for terminally ill patients in the comfort of their own homes.

Infusion

A nurse specializing in infusions administers medications, fluids, and blood to patients through intravenous injection, often in a catheter or port for those patients who will be on long-term care. The boundaries of this type of nursing can be blurred with the home-care nurse or the hospice nurse, as infusions offering pain relief and comfort for the terminally ill are common.

Long-Term Care

Nurses specializing in long-term care provide care to patients with chronic physical or mental disorders or diseases. Long-term care brings with it its own unique challenges and idiosyncracies, and the nurse specializing in long-term care gains experience dealing with these challenges.

Medical-Surgical Nurse

The medical-surgical nurse provides care to patients mostly in clinical and hospital settings. The surgical nurse becomes specialized in sterile procedures and maintaining the sterile environment of the surgical suite.

Occupational Health Nurse

This unique type of nursing treats job-related injuries and illnesses. These medical professionals help employers in detecting workplace hazards and help them determine how to implement health and safety standards issued by OSHA and other workplace-related regulators.

Perianesthesia Nurses

Specializing in anesthesia, these nurses provide preoperative and postoperative care to patients undergoing anesthesia during surgery.

Other

There is a huge list of other specialties in which RNs work, including:

- *Disease-specific nurse.* Focuses on diabetes management, addiction care, HIV-AIDS, oncology, genetics screening and caring for patients with genetic disorders such as cystic fibrosis or Huntington's disease. These nurses provide care in many different settings, including homes, institutions, clinics, and hospitals.

- *Nurse practitioner.* Provides basic primary health care, including in some states, diagnosing illnesses and prescribing medications.

- *Organ or body system-specific nurse.* Cardiac, dermatology, nephrology (kidney), ophthalmic, and respiratory, for example, working in all different kinds of settings.

- *Perioperative nurse.* Assists surgeons by selecting and handing instruments, controlling bleeding, and suturing incisions.

- *Public health nurse.* Works in government and private facilities instructing families, individuals, and groups on health issues, disease prevention, and nutrition, as well as working in schools and other community health education settings.

- *Occupational nurse.* Provides nursing care at workplaces.
- *Population-specific nurse.* Neonatal (newborns), children (pediatrics), and elderly (geriatrics), for example.
- *Radiologic nurse.* Provides care to patients undergoing diagnostic radiation procedures.
- *Transplant nurse.* Cares for transplant recipients and living donors.
- *Traveling nurse.* Works as long-term temporary staff members in locations as needed throughout the country, which requires lots of relocation.

Some nurses have jobs that require little or no direct patient contact. Most of these positions still require an active RN license. They include:

- *Case managers.* Ensure that all of the medical needs of patients with severe injuries and illnesses are met, including the type, location, and duration of treatment.
- *Forensics nurses.* Combine nursing with law enforcement by treating and investigating victims of sexual assault, child abuse, or accidental death.
- *Infection control nurses.* Identify, track, and control infectious outbreaks in health care facilities, as well as develop methods of outbreak prevention, biological terrorism responses, and staff immunization clinics.
- *Legal nurse consultants.* Assist lawyers in medical cases by interviewing patients and witnesses, organizing

medical records, determining damages and costs, locating evidence, and educating lawyers about medical issues.

- *Nurse administrators.* Supervise nursing staff, establish work schedules and budgets, and maintain medical supply inventories.
- *Nurse educators.* Teach student nurses and also provide continuing education for RNs.
- *Nurse informaticists.* Collect, store, and analyze nursing data in order to improve efficiency, reduce risk, and improve patient care.

RNs also may work as health care consultants, public policy advisors, pharmaceutical and medical supply researchers and salespersons, and medical writers and editors.

Nursing is clearly a field that is as diverse or as specialized as you want to make it.

Specialized and
Higher-Level Work
in Health Care

PROFILE

Mary Bensen
Occupational Therapist

By the time she graduated from high school, Mary Bensen had received so much physical therapy for sports injuries that she decided she wanted to be a physical therapist. But because she applied to the University of New England a little late, there were no openings left in physical therapy. The school suggested she enter as an occupational therapy (OT) major and transfer to physical therapy (PT) before the end of two years.

"My intention was definitely to move into PT, but I ended up loving OT. There is a much broader scope of what you can do."

To become an OT, Mary earned a bachelor's degree and did a six-month internship. These days, most OTs get master's degrees.

Mary's first job was with New England Rehabilitation Hospital, where she knew she would get exposure to the most diverse cases. New England Rehab worked with the largest Maine hospital, Maine Medical Center; Mary worked with its spinal cord injury team, got experience working with amputees, and she ran a therapeutic horseback riding program (her horse experience resonated with the person hiring, which Mary thinks is what got her the job to begin with).

Hospitals are eager to hire new graduates, Mary found, because they can pay them lower wages than experienced OTs. She was working too hard, too many hours, and for too little money. So she left and took a position as rehab manager at a home for the elderly.

"I found it hard," she says, "because the patients didn't really want to do the therapy." Mary left there to work in home health care.

After working in home health, Mary left Maine and took an intriguing job in Connecticut for a company that made helmets for babies born with misshapen heads. This job, she says, was fascinating. She got to watch amazing surgeries, cast children's heads for the helmets before they were even out of anesthesia, and she traveled a lot.

Eventually, her kids got homesick for their grandparents and she returned to Maine. This time Mary took a position in a school—but left that when she realized the job involved more paperwork than treatment.

But throughout her work meanderings, Mary landed on the kind of occupational therapy she was really interested in—pediatrics. She now works basically for herself, doing outpatient occupational therapy in a pediatric office.

Mary works with all ages of children. She has a two-week old patient coming in who has separated clavicles. She will do positioning and teach the parents how to do it. She will probably follow this child throughout the next few months, making sure he makes his developmental milestones. She works with a pair of twins who have neck muscle problems, probably from the lack of space in the womb, and a 17-year-old stroke victim who has lingering arm/hand weakness. She also works with autistic children. This is the kind of diversity Mary loves about her work as an occupational therapist.

She feels her schooling at UNE prepared her well for her job. Despite the lack of daily interaction with OT colleagues in her self-employed capacity, she calls on a former professor who works in a pediatric clinic run by UNE when she needs to consult a colleague.

Mary has seen the profession blossom in the last 13 years, in no small part due to the fact that physicians are much more willing to prescribe OT and better understand its benefits.

How does Mary feel about her career choice?

"I am very happy with my decision," she says.

■ ■ ■

The jobs in this chapter are those that are off-the-beaten-path because of their relatively new entry into health care, such as medical billing experts, those that have been around a while but are somewhat atypical health care professions, and some others that have been around a while have benefits that have become more generally accepted, such as Mary Bensen's occupational therapy work. Some of them require training as a nurse or are jobs that a nursing background can help you move into. Most require a certain amount of specialized training specifically for that job.

Medical Billing Specialist

Anyone who has had even the simplest medical procedure in the last 20 years can understand how important this job is. With multiple insurance providers and bills from several different practitioners, medical billing is complex at best.

Start Your Health Care Career

You need decent math skills and an ability to pay close attention to detail to be a medical billing specialist even in the smallest health care office. Each procedure has a code which must be attached to the procedure on the bill. The patient's insurance company matches all of the codes. Because insurance companies are looking for any excuse to delay payment, these codes need to be right or the insurance company will deny the claim and bump it back to the doctor's office without payment.

Your workday as a medical billing specialist will probably be nine-to-five. Depending on the size of the office, you may also take care of other financial matters. Even if you already have an accounting degree, you will probably need to take courses specifically in medical billing at one of the many training schools around the country.

Patient Advocate

The health care industry continues to get more and more complicated. Patients no longer simply go to their local hospital. The entire country and, in some cases the world, has become the hospital in your backyard. With such complexity, it is difficult for most patients to take care of ensuring that they are getting the right care. In comes the patient advocate.

This field is relatively new and fast becoming an important part of the health care world. Patient advocates help patients in the health care system sort out questions they have about their care and help them receive the best health care they can. Advocates help with questions on procedures, sit with patients during medical visits to act as that important second set of ears to hear and interpret what the doctor is saying to the patient, and help patients get second opinions. Advocates accompany patients to the hospital and help ensure the right procedure is done to the right body part and that patients get the post-operative care they need. And through it all, they help with sorting out the billing and making sure insurance covers what it should.

People who can afford to pay for a patient advocate can choose anyone they want to help them. Nonprofits, like the Patient Advocate Foundation, also help patients to weave their way through the health care system. They also lobby the federal government on bills and legislation that is designed to further assist patients.

Although patient advocacy is not necessarily yet fully accepted by the health care industry, some hospitals are starting to offer such services. To be a patient advocate, it is helpful to have a nursing degree or other certification in the health care field.

Chiropractor

The chiropractic field has become much more accepted in the medical industry over the past few decades. There was a time when chiropractors were not thought of as real doctors. And while it is true they are not practicing medicine in the classic physician manner, chiropractors go through rigorous training to become certified to practice.

The chiropractor focuses his or her efforts around the spine, in the belief that misalignment of the spine distorts the nervous system's smooth flow and contributes to a host of health problems—a so-called holistic approach to medicine. One of the fundamental principles of chiropractics is that the human body is an organism capable of sustaining and maintaining its own health. The focus, therefore, is on enhancing the body's immune system.

To work as a Doctor of Chiropractic, you must be certified by passing national boards and be a graduate of an accredited school. You need an undergraduate degree first. If you want to expedite your chiropractic degree, you would be wise to take plenty of science classes in your undergrad work. You need to go into the chiropractic program with chemistry, organic chemistry, physics, anatomy, physiology, and perhaps a few other science classes under your belt. If you don't have those credits on your transcript, you need to get them before you can enter chiropractic school.

Then it's on to a four-year program that encompasses internships working in the field. Palmer College of Chiropractic, started by the founder of chiropractics, Daniel David Palmer, and now with three locations—the original in Iowa, in Florida, and in California—is the premier chiropractic school in the United States although there are now many excellent schools.

Life as a chiropractor can be as different as you want to make it. A practice specializing in personal injury is probably going to be fully reliant on insurance and will need to see patients in relatively short time frames as the insurance company dictates care. The other approach to chiropractics is to start or join a family practice. You can take more time with patients and get to know their lifestyle, attitudes, stress levels, and other things that contribute to their overall well being.

You will be on your feet much of the time. You need to have a certain amount of strength to perform chiropractic procedures, especially as you have no control over the size of your patients. They may be petite to overweight, young or elderly, and muscular or more frail. Depending on your personal desires, you can either open your own practice, buy into and run your own practice, or work in the practice of another chiropractor.

Dietitian

A registered dietitian (RD) requires an intense education with a science emphasis, an education received through an American Dietetic Association (ADA)-accredited program. Dietitians advise patients on maintaining health and managing disease at least in part through diet. In order to do this, they need to understand the complex chemical makeup of foods and how they contribute to health and body tissue maintenance and repair.

Dietitians must be registered, a process overseen by the American Dietetic Association (www.eatright.org). They must pass a national exam, and many states also require licensing.

Dietitians can be generalists and work in schools, hospitals, and other institutions helping with food selection and with general patient care. They can also, through continued education, specialize in areas from pediatrics to geriatrics, renal care, oncology, and other conditions. Perhaps one of the largest areas of growth for dietitians has been in diabetes care.

The American Dietetic Association is a well-established organization that supports dietitians. It provides public information, and many of its dietitians serve as media liaisons, getting accurate information to the public via broadcast and print media.

Helping people maintain healthy lifestyles and learn healthy eating habits can be rewarding. Because dietitians work closely with patients, they need to have good interpersonal skills, relate well to others, and be empathetic to many different types of people and lifestyles.

As in nursing, the great majority of RDs are women. Because most of the work in the dietetic field is institutional, the work conditions would be those of hospitals or long-term care institutions. Some RDs also make a good living doing consulting.

Nuclear Medicine Technologist

Nuclear medicine has been an up-and-coming area of medical diagnostics for several years. The number of nuclear medical technologists needed is not great, so the job opportunities are not huge; those who combine other types of diagnostic testing skills will be the best suited for finding work.

The nuclear medicine technologist typically prepares and administers nuclear preparations to the patient. The tech then tracks the radioactive material as it travels through the patient's body using special scanning cameras and captures certain images along the way according to instructions from the doctor.

Work as a nuclear medicine technologist requires you to be on your feet most of the day as you operate the camera and readjust patients as required for various image views. Patients may be disabled and wheelchair-bound and may require a certain amount of strength to move. This work also requires considerable computer use.

Other types of nuclear medicine, such as a radioactive compound used to treat hyperthyroidism or in laboratory procedures, do not involve imaging. These still require intense regulation.

Although you could become a skilled nuclear medicine technologist with on-the-job training, you would be better off going through formal training and getting certification. This would ensure you are learning the very latest in safety training, and you learn valuable information regarding camera positioning for the best diagnosis. These programs are available throughout the country and are usually one or perhaps two years long.

All work as a nuclear medicine technologist is under the strict supervision of a nuclear medicine physician. The physician reviews cases, orders the diagnostics, prescribes the amount of medicine to be used, and diagnoses based on the results of the testing.

Nuclear medicine is almost exclusively performed in hospitals. Salaries are fairly good, in the mid-to-upper $40s, and include some hazard pay—and some hazards. Any medical personnel working with radioactivity of any kind, from nuclear medicine to x-rays, are required to wear a radioactive monitoring badge which gets sent to a lab once a month to test radioactivity exposure. Your place of employment receives a report once a month; your supervisor will notify you if you are over the limit and will help you learn safer techniques in use of lead shields and gloves and other safety precautions.

Although nuclear medicine poses some risk of additional exposure, if properly protected, your exposure should be considerably less than you get just walking outside on a sunny day.

Occupational Therapist (OT)

Occupational therapy (OT), a fast-growing field, helps people improve or recover their ability to perform tasks in their daily living and working environments. They work with individuals who are mentally, physically, developmentally, or emotionally disabled. Occupational therapists help clients not only to improve their basic motor functions and reasoning abilities, but also find ways to help them to compensate for permanent loss of function. The overall goal of occupational therapists is to help clients have independent, productive, and satisfying lives.

They help people learn to effectively and safely operate wheelchairs, stair lifts, and even just a simple cane or walker— including how to get themselves in and out of vehicles. Occupational therapists may also collaborate with patients and employers to modify the work environment so that people with disabilities can work.

Some occupational therapists specialize in certain groups of individuals, such as by age or by type of disability. They also sometimes work with groups, facilitating listening and social interaction skills. And the elderly benefit greatly from occupational therapy, helping to alleviate falls or function with severe arthritis in the hands.

Occupational therapists typically work the usual 40-hour week, with some need for nights and weekends, especially for those OTs working outside the institutional setting. Median annual incomes are in the mid $50s.

Starting in 2007, occupational therapists need to have completed a master's degree to practice and have at least six months of supervised work in the field. States regulate the occupational therapist practice; all states require passing of a national exam.

Occupational therapists work in a variety of settings, from hospitals to nursing homes to private homes and offices, making this a rewarding health care field with work as varied as you like. And it's not going away any time soon, the field will be growing at least for the next several years.

Social Worker

To be a successful social worker, you really must enjoy helping people. Social workers often see people in dire situations, with employment, housing, personal, or family problems that are often the result of substance abuse, serious illness, or disability.

Social workers can specialize in a variety of areas—helping with adoptions, working with domestic abuse situations, or looking out for child welfare. Two areas of growth are working with the expanding elderly population and working with substance abuse clients who are more and more frequently being treated through nonprison arrangements. Although they may regularly travel locally to visit clients, social workers spend most of their time in an office.

Social work can be a high pressure job. You need to be the kind of person who knows how to relieve stress and be able to separate from your work when you leave the office. Otherwise, it can be too emotionally draining. Burnout is a big factor in this field.

Like other fields in health care these days, a bachelor's degree in social work is sufficient but the industry preference is leaning heavily toward a master's degree. The undergraduate degree will still get you an entry-level position, but to do more advanced social work, be in management or other supervisory positions, or to get a job in certain agencies will require the graduate degree. There are several governing bodies for social work and licensing requirements vary from state to state.

Most social workers work in the urban environment, many for government-run agencies, although private practice is a possibility. The social work field is expected to grow. While hospitals are releasing patients sooner than ever before, often cutting patients off from the in-hospital social work assistance, at-home social work is becoming more prevalent.

Average salary for social workers in 2004, according to the U.S. Department of Labor, was in the mid $30s, with higher salaries coming from the hospital setting.

Emergency Medical Technician (EMT)

If you like the adrenalin rush of being called to duty in the middle of the night to be among the first responders to all manner of life-and-death emergencies, EMT is the job for you.

The basis for the EMT is the fire department, police department, or local rescue squad, and this will continue to be the case. There are few private ambulance services, but those communities that do support them will need EMTs. While EMTs have long been mostly volunteer, that is changing as volunteers are replaced by paid staff, especially in urban and suburban areas.

Training is vital. Those who have nursing degrees make great EMTs—not only do they have training in nursing procedures, but nurses in general tend to have a matter-of-fact attitude that allows them to dig in and help with what needs to be done in a crisis. EMT is not a job for procrastinators.

Advanced training, either as an RN or other EMT-specific training, allows you to perform procedures as the patient is on the way to the hospital. Sometimes doctors direct the EMT by radio or phone as the ambulance is en route to the hospital.

You need to be willing to be on call at least a portion of the time. Accidents do not happen only nine to five. EMT can be another burnout field, so you need to be good at managing your stress load.

According to the U.S. Department of Labor, there are four levels of emergency personnel in the National Registry of Emergency Medical Technicians: First Responder, EMT-Basic, EMT-Intermediate, and EMT-Paramedic. The paramedic leads the pack with the ability to carry out the most advanced emergency care. Many states also have their own registration requirements.

These days, the basic educational requirement for an EMT is a 110- to 120-hour program that includes practice in specific emergency situations such as treating shock, clearing airway obstructions, use of backboards, and emergency births. And you can continue your training from there.

The work conditions for the EMT are not considered spectacular. There is definitely heavy lifting involved, exposure to communicable diseases, and work environments in any weather that can be imagined, depending on where you live. Work hours are also long, averaging 50 a week in most work situations. Average salaries are low, in the mid-$20s, and the high side—which represents less than 10 percent of all EMTs—is in the mid-$40s.

All that said, EMT work can be the most satisfying health care-related work you can do.

Medical Transcriptionist

In this growing field, medical transcriptionists listen to dictated recordings made by physicians and other health care professionals and transcribe them into medical reports, correspondence, and other administrative material. Like most transcription work, the transcriber listens to a recording on a headset and keys the text into a computer. The documents produced by a medical transcription service include discharge summaries, history and physical examination reports, operative reports, consultation reports, autopsy reports, diagnostic imaging studies, progress notes, and referral letters. The documents are returned to the physician or other health care professional who dictated them for review and signature, or correction. These documents eventually become part of patients' permanent files.

As a medical transcriptionist, you need to understand medical terminology, anatomy and physiology, diagnostic procedures, pharmacology, and treatment assessments as well as translate medical jargon and abbreviations into their fully expanded forms. You must know the standards that apply to the style of medical records as well as legal and ethical requirements involved with keeping patient information confidential.

The advance of speech recognition technology is changing this field considerably. One appealing aspect of being a medical transcriptionist is that many work from home offices. Others may work in a physician's office as a secretary or administrative assistant, doing other jobs at the same time.

Work hazards include the usual ones of anyone sitting at a computer for long periods of time: back strain, eye strain, tendonitis, and carpal tunnel syndrome. It is important to take precautions against these disorders. Average hourly wage, according to the U.S. Department of Labor, was about $13.50 in 2004. Pay methods vary from hourly to by-line to hourly with bonuses for rapid turnaround or simply by project. There are associate's degree programs available to become a medical transcriptionist.

■　■　■

This is in no way an exhaustive list of off-the-beaten-path job opportunities in the medical world. An afternoon on the internet and a few conversations with other health care professionals and you can definitely come up with something that you probably didn't even know existed and that will capture your imagination.

CHAPTER 7

The Working
Environment

PROFILE
Kathy Bird
Nurse

After getting her BS in nursing, Kathy Bird worked for about three years as a medical surgical nurse and in pediatrics. Then she went to graduate school to be a pediatric nurse practitioner. She worked in primary care pediatrics for an HMO health clinic for four years, where she performed physicals and visited sick patients from ages birth to 22. She also did newborn discharges at hospitals. Of the three nurses in her clinic, she was the only female, so she got a following of adolescent female patients. This led to work in eating disorders.

When her husband was transferred to the U.S. Virgin Islands, Kathy continued her career. There she did a combination of pediatrics and emergency work on things such as sickle cell anemia, jellyfish sting bites, and near drownings. And Kathy saw lots of rashes, an eclectic variety, very different from the rashes seen on the mainland. She found that she enjoyed diagnosing rashes, which led to an interest in dermatology. Previous ER work had helped prepare Kathy for the surgical procedures required in dermatology repair.

One thing that Kathy has seen change over the years is that the nursing profession has gotten more organized. With all the education she has pursued, why did Kathy choose nursing over becoming an MD? She admits the money, while good, is not as good as that of an MD, but she appreciates the nursing field's focus on wellness and teaching people to be healthy. In addition, you can come out of school ready to practice sooner than if you were pursuing an MD license; and you can have time to have a family.

Kathy's HMO work helped her in feeling her way through to her chosen aspect of her health career. "I worked in psychiatry, orthopedics, sports medicine. I would go spend a day and a half to do rotation with different specialists."

When Kathy returned the the United States from the Virgin Islands, she worked with a female dermatologist for eight years until her employer decided to take early retirement.

The most frustrating part of her work now is outside restrictions that prevent her from giving patients the exact advice and recommendations she might like. In Massachusetts where she practices, the AMA restricts the nurse practitioner to practice under a physician, although in 12 other states a nurse practitioner can have her or his own practice.

Kathy's advice to those entering the health care field is to keep checking things out and advancing. Keep your eyes open because there are opportunities everywhere. And some interest like Kathy's in dermatology, may crop up when you least expect it.

■   ■   ■

The diversity of the health care field brings with it a great diversity when it comes to the working environment. You can basically work in any kind of environment you choose, depending on what kind of health care job most appeals to you or suits your background. Your day-to-day work life can involve people or not, colleagues or not, standing all day, sitting all day, being on the road, or spending the day in one room. It really just depends on your own choices, such as those Kathy Bird made, taking her into the emergency environment, the hospital arena, and private practice offices.

Lifestyle, Culture, and Attitudes

Like all industries, health care comes with its own personalities. But, health care is a little different because the circumstance of work life can be so varied.

Caretaking

First and foremost, the health care industry tends to be full of people who have a natural tendency toward caretaking. Although the trend toward mostly female nurses has changed, women in their natural hands-on caretaking role continue to be a main component of the nursing part of the industry.

Compassion

Nursing professionals with just a few years of experience behind them have seen it all. They are fully aware that a health crisis can happen to anyone at any time. Empathy is a critical trait of the health care worker.

They also often have a natural tendency to want to teach patients—about their condition, about self-care, and about living with their condition or getting through the rough parts. Nursing professionals need to have the ability to teach in a way that is not condescending or presumptive; they know that it is important for their patients to not feel defensive and end up unwilling to listen to advice and instruction.

Dedication

Depending on the part of the health care world you get into, the hours can be long and intense. There is a dedication among health care workers, especially in the hands-on part of the industry, to be focused on the well-being of their patients. Many will go above and beyond the call of duty, especially in hospice care and lesser-funded, lower-staffed clinics that care for lower-income patients or those without health insurance.

Even Temperament

Working with the public in any field requires a grit-your-teeth ability that allows you to deal with different personality types. And in the medical field you may find that you are often dealing with people when they are not at their best. If you can maintain an even temperament through even the worst of scenes, you can disarm disgruntled patients, calm anxious patients, and help keep things cool with all of your colleagues.

Eye for Detail

The medical field is an exact science in most ways. Drug administration, performing sterile procedures—these are not "the best you can do" types of jobs. These things need to be done perfectly. Another place where an eye for detail is critical is in assisting a surgeon—keeping tabs on what the surgeon is doing and anticipating what he or she might need next is the sign of a good assistant.

Multi-Tasking

Nursing and other medical professions require you to be able to do many things at once—keep a patient calm, comfortable, and informed; perform a procedure; and listen to a doctor or give instructions to an assistant may be things you are juggling at the same time. Busy practices with multiple providers have numerous patients in the office at the same time. Multitasking is a skill that most people in the health care profession might want to become proficient at.

Tolerance

Nurses see AIDs patients, teenage mothers, people of all races and religious beliefs. The health care profession needs to be one of tolerance for other people's lifestyles and beliefs.

The profession itself is made up of people from all nationalities. The United States is a key destination, especially for those seeking to become doctors.

Learning a foreign language or two can be helpful, both in communicating well with your colleagues and, depending upon your location, in interacting with patients. Knowing more than one language can also open up opportunities to work in other countries.

Ethics

The medical industry is highly regulated by state and government agencies. It is critical to operate with the highest ethical standards. As in any industry, you may well run across the office that does not follow that creed. If you find yourself in that environment, it would be best to move on. Whether you report such a finding to authorities is up to you, but you should definitely remove yourself from connection with less-than-ethical practices.

The Workplace and the Working Pace

The actual workplace for the health care worker comes in almost every flavor and depends greatly on what area of the industry you choose.

If you work on the health insurance side or in a billing department of a large hospital or as a receptionist in a large multi-provider practice, you will be working in a normal office environment sitting behind a desk, probably working on a computer and answering the phone much of the time. The working pace will probably be comfortably busy, without a lot of time to be bored.

The nightshift nurse in an inner city emergency room, on the other hand, has almost a completely opposite work life from the office environment. You will be on your feet a lot. You probably will need to do some heavy lifting and deal with some less-than-cooperative patients. The working pace will be busy and perhaps a bit more on the frantic side, at least at times.

Hours

The health care field also offers the worker the possibility of all sorts of hours, suiting almost anyone's personal preference. Shift work is common especially among nursing staff, either in hospitals or home care. On-call requirements vary according to the area of care you are in, but if you are doing home care, expect to be required to be on call some part of each month.

Many workers in the health care industry are on part-time schedules. According to the U.S. Department of Labor statistics, part-time workers made up about 20 percent of the workforce as a whole in 2004, but accounted for 39 percent of workers in offices of dentists and 33 percent of those in offices of other health practitioners. Students, parents with young children, dual jobholders, and older workers make up much of the part-time workforce, according to the USDL web site.

This variety of working hours makes health care a desire-able career choice for people with many different lifestyles. Two-career couples can arrange for one parent to work a nine-to-five job while the other parent works a night shift in the health care industry, leaving a parent always home for young children.

Injury

Many nursing workers can also expect to do some heavy lifting. You will need to learn the best body mechanics for avoiding injury. Most offices will teach you this or at least have manuals and charts to help you learn how to lift with your knees and other best practices. And if you went to nursing school, you will have learned this in a clinical methods classes. According to the U.S. Department of Labor, health care workers involved in direct patient care must take precautions to prevent back strain from lifting patients and equipment; to minimize exposure to radiation and caustic chemicals; and to guard against infectious diseases, such as AIDS, tuberculosis, and hepatitis. Home care personnel who make house calls are exposed to the possibility of being injured in highway accidents, all types of overexertion when assisting patients, and falls inside and outside homes.

These risks mean the industry average for occupational injury and illness is higher than the overall averages. It's 5.0 for workers in all occupations compared to 8.7 per 100 for workers in the hospital environment. And nursing care facility worker injury rates are even higher.

Stress

Stress can be part of many careers. Health care certainly is one where work stress is an issue. Stress can be controlled simply by the career path you choose—some parts of the health care industry are more naturally stress-inducing than others. For instance, you can imagine probably from personal experience that working in an urban emergency room is fast-paced. But working, say, as an RN or LPN in the infectious diseases office at a small-town hospital is probably not too stress-inducing— but that is different from person to person.

You need to figure out ways to keep a handle on your stress level. Any doctor will tell you that stress is a natural life occurrence, and some stress is a good thing. It keeps us on our toes, make us feel alive. But too much stress—which is different for everyone—can lead to health problems. You may find yourself picking up every little disease that comes through your clinic. Stress overload can compromise your immune system enough to make your body vulnerable to illness.

Too much stress can cause tenseness in your muscles and therefore be an inadvertent cause of back sprain, shoulder strain, and other temporarily debilitating problems. Excess stress can cause headaches, digestive disorders, allergic reactions, and a multitude of other things that may not at first seem related.

Good old-fashioned exercise is one great stress reliever. If your workplace offers a gym or discounted admission to a fitness center, make use of it. People relieve stress in many different ways—a nice meal with colleagues, the occasional long weekend vacation, a Sunday afternoon matinee of a newly released movie, or the occasional "mental health day" all can go a long way to helping you unwind.

Sometimes a job change is in order. Some people find shift work to be stressful. Others find nine-to-five a grind and get stressed out from being bored. If you like your work environment overall, talk with your supervisor about possibilities for relieving stress without leaving your employer. Maybe you can change your shift, work in a different area of the hospital, or change your on-call schedule.

It's important to figure out what your stress level parameters are and to take care of stress before it causes you problems. If you are unable to come to work, you are unable to do what most people in health care like doing the most—taking care of other people.

Co-Workers

If you go into nursing, your co-workers will be 94 percent female. Recent statistics from the Center for Nursing Advocacy show an extremely slowly increasing number of male nurses, now at around 6 percent of the nursing workforce. Workplace empowerment, poor relations with physicians, lack of physician respect, and major communication breakdowns are all cited a problems for nurses. These things are thought to be less tolerated by men than women, making men who do become nurses more likely to leave the profession, keeping the statistics low.

Some other health care professions are a little less unbalanced, although professions like dietitian, diabetes educator, and many others are still in great part filled by women.

The field is, however, diverse in its age brackets, with many new young graduates as well as older women returning to the workplace.

Building a
Resume

When Eva Ramone moved, she needed to leave her job in the book publishing industry and find something in the new city where she was headed. She accepted a position as executive assistant to the CEO of a hospital in a small Maine city.

Eva spends most of her day at the computer or on the phone scheduling meetings and arranging travel. She sees a lot of people, but they are people coming in for meetings. Rarely does she run across the medical staff, although the ones she has met seem like wonderful people that are very compassionate and caring.

In fact, the only times that Eva gets a sense of being in the medical environment is when she hears ambulance sirens. The hospital also announces the birth of a baby by playing chimes over the PA system—a very nice touch, Eva thinks.

The position of executive assistant, Eva says, comes with high expectations. The job is to do everything you can to make the executive you work for look his or her best. Eva describes her salary as a little better than average for a job in the area.

Eva works 7:30 to 4, hours she chose. The benefits at the hospital are good, but because she was hired as a long-term temporary position, she doesn't qualify. The hospital offers few paid holidays as it is always open. There is free parking that is scattered around the surrounding neighborhoods; the hospital provides a shuttle service. And, Eva says, employees get a generous discount to eat in the hospital cafeteria, and the food is excellent and varied.

Compared to publishing, however, Eva finds the environment to be one of constant tension. She had never thought of health care as an industry she was interested in and hasn't found any other aspects of the industry appeal to her. In fact, although she has found the job interesting, she has decided she will not stay and is currently looking for a new job.

■ ■ ■

Many ways exist to build a resume in the health care setting—Eva Ramone was able to test the waters of the medical environment simply by having a strong work ethic, office experience, and excellent references. It is important to think about where you want your career to go. One of the best ways to do that is to go out in the field and work. You can plunge in and get a job—although without any formal schooling the job you get will probably not pay a living wage. Depending on your circumstances, you may have to explore the field with a side job. You can also do volunteer work to gain experience.

Resume Fundamentals

Your resume is usually the first view a potential employer has of you and your suitability to the job and the company. It is basically an outline of your career-related history, with a little spice included, personal interests.

What's On It

A resume can include many things:

- *Education*, including where/when you graduated from high school, if/when you graduated from college; any graduate work you have done; and any other education you have pursued such as seminars and workshops, especially those for which you received CEUs.

- *Work history* as far back as is applicable to your age and the position for which you are applying. In other words, if you are 22, it would be appropriate to include what you did for summer work in high school, especially if it is applicable to the job you want; if you are 42, your resume probably should not include your high school years.

- *Volunteer work* should definitely cover be covered completely, with things you have done as far back as is appropriate or fits on your resume (see below for length recommendations). Volunteering is proof you are willing to go above and beyond the call of duty, that you are a good community citizen, and is often indicative of your interests.

- *Personal information* is not necessary on a resume but often can pique the interest of the person reviewing dozens of resumes and provide an icebreaker in an interview. For instance, indicating you knit or restore classic cars or teach sculpting to high school kids can be a topic of conversation that an interviewer can use to help you relax before you begin talking about the nitty gritty of the job. Don't include every little thing you are interested in or every detail about your personal life—usually if you have children and a couple hobbies is sufficient. But do include anything that might be relevant to the job for which you are applying, such as that you spent the past decade caring for your brother with cerebral palsy.

- *Career goals or objectives* were once integral to a resume but they need to be carefully worded so they don't exclude you from being considered even before you get an interview. Best thing may be to leave this out.

- *Publications list* should always be included with your resume. If you are highly published and the list is long, you might want to list a generic count (over 100 articles in medical journals and six books). When you go that route, offer to send a complete publications list on request.

- *Professional memberships* can be worth mentioning, especially ones specifically related to the industry in which the job you are applying falls.

- *References* are often listed as "available on request." This way when an employer requests references you get a head's up that he or she is seriously considering you. This also allows you to tailor the references you provide to the job for which you are applying.

Length

As short as possible. That's the answer to the question, "How long should my resume be?" How short is that? For people early in their careers, one page is the absolute maximum. For people in mid-career, two pages is sufficient. For people with complex management careers or later in their work lives, you might be able to squeak it to three pages without looking like you are writing your autobiography (and expecting people to read it).

If you are early in your career and have had so many jobs that you need four pages for your resume, you don't want to flaunt that. List your jobs chronologically from recent to history and plan to explain any gaps if you decide to leave out those two years that you skipped around at different restaurant jobs.

And don't write four paragraphs about each job. Keep your job descriptions to one or two sentences—you need to leave something to talk about in your interview. Put down enough to explain what you did and intrigue your potential employer, but not so much that they don't know what they would talk with you about if you came in.

The Language

When you write your job history, use the key language that is used in the advertisement. Some phrases you will run across in health care are:

- efficiency management
- multitasking
- excellent communications skills
- bilingual a plus

- billing experience
- works well under pressure
- team player

Look for these kinds of phrases in the ads you are responding to and tailor your resume to address them. Highlight jobs that, for instance, would point to your ability to be a team player or to your success in working under pressure.

Resume Style

Resumes can be done in whatever style you like the best. Books abound that show different resume styles, especially when you progress to a higher level in your job search. Also, most word processing software comes with resume templates that you can use.

Two common styles are (1) to list your work history chronologically from most recent back, or (2) to segment your resume into skills such as "team building," "management," or "multitasking" and list job history relevant to those skills.

Whatever style you decide to use, keep your resume simple and make sure the most pertinent information is easily found. Use basic fonts like Times New Roman or Bookman Old Style, and use emphasis in the form of italics, boldface, and underlining with discretion—use too much of it and it doesn't emphasize anything. And use a font size between 10 and 12, large enough to read but not so large it looks like your resume is in large print for the visually impaired.

Make your name, address, and other contact information a key element in the design of your resume. You want it to be easy for potential employers to see who you are and how to get in touch with you for an interview.

Finally

Use your spellcheck on your resume and also have a good proofreader read it each time you update it. And update it as often as necessary. In the past, resumes were typed on a typewriter and printed 100 copies at a time at an offset printer. These days, keep a resume folder on your computer and update the resume every time something significant happens in your career—you receive an award, a degree, a license, get published, and certainly when you get settled into a new job.

Be careful when you update your resume that you don't disrupt the format of your resume. This can be a pain to readjust.

E-mail resumes when required, but otherwise it is best to send them good, old-fashioned snail mail or other courier. Format of a resume sent by e-mail can get all discombobulated, ruining all your hard work. Also, a faxed resume, while quick, can look terrible on the other end and even have parts that are hard to read, especially numbers—important ones like your phone number. If you have to e-mail or fax a resume, follow up if appropriate with a mailed one on quality stationery.

Volunteering

Volunteering is a great way to get firsthand experience in health care. By volunteering you can help figure out what area of health care appeals to you and you can get real experience to put on your resume. It also shows a serious commitment when you take your own time to get involved in a field you are considering.

Hospitals

Many aspects of health care allow for a volunteer opportunity. One that provides the most is the hospital setting. Nonprofit hospitals especially tend to have a range of volunteer possibilities.

Hospital volunteers have traditionally been called "candy stripers" because they were identified as volunteers by wearing a pink-and-white striped uniform. Not all volunteers wear the candy-stripe uniform, which tend to be reserved for high school-aged volunteers.

Small hospitals often have volunteer greeters at the front desk who provide a welcoming face to visitors and help them find the room of the patient they are visiting. They also often work in hospital libraries and resource rooms, helping patients and other users find materials, make photocopies, and use computers.

Pet therapy has become popular in hospitals. This is usually done by volunteers who bring their calm, friendly dogs in to make the rounds, visit patients, and help cheer them up.

Individual hospitals offer other types of volunteer possibilities, so it is a good place to start to become familiar with health care as a potential career.

Non-Hospital Settings

Nursing homes, children's hospitals, blood drives, and free screening clinics are also always looking for volunteers. You can read to patients, check in blood donors, and see all sorts of different types of settings in the health care industry.

EMT

Another big volunteer opportunity in health care is to become an emergency medical technician (EMT) for your local ambulance service, especially in smaller towns. Ambulances in most towns are run by the fire department. Talk with the fire chief to find out how to become involved in your town.

Becoming an EMT can be time-consuming and expensive, and it can require a significant commitment, depending on where you live. It will require you take a class. Some departments have the finances or receive state or federal grants to help EMTs pay for the required training.

EMT work is demanding and requires a certain personality type—you definitely need to be able to work under pressure.

Nurses are often involved in lifesquad or EMT, and nursing experience can be very useful. But there are many other volunteer opportunities with the ambulance service that are less stressful and less hands-on, such as driving the ambulance. You need, of course, to be a good driver with a clean driving record. You are still in a pressure situation, but this job does not require the medical skills of the EMT and other personnel delivering help at the scene.

Some ambulance services are short on volunteers. If they have the room in the ambulance, they appreciate an extra hand to call dispatch, help with the patient's family, or whatever else comes up.

This kind of work can give you a close-up view of what life in an ER might be like. And it is great experience to put on your resume.

Internships

Most licensing programs for any health care job require you go out into the field and do hands-on work in the clinical setting. In fact, they typically dictate a certain number of required hours to pass the program, usually coordinated after you have completed certain appropriate classes.

Don't take these internships lightly. Go to different places and check out what it might be like to do an internship there before you make a decision. Think about what you want to accomplish at this stage in your decision-making process. Keep in mind where you are in your education and understand that if this is the first of two internships you are required to do, you won't be learning everything you need to know how to the first time around.

These internships can be great in helping you get experience in possible aspects of health care that you might be interested.

Part-Time Work

If you are considering health care as a career change, working part time in a health care setting is one way to get a feel for the field. And it is a great addition to your resume.

Although much of the part-time work available in health care settings requires licensing or certification, if you are willing to answer phones, do filing, or do other entry-level work, you can still build your resume with real experience and get a view from the inside. You can learn a lot from a book like this one, but no book will compare to the insight you get as you drive home from a shift in a busy ER on whether you could deal with that environment on a day-to-day basis.

Outside of Health Care

There is other work you can do that will help you build a resume suitable for a job in health care. Even if you plan to get licensed as a dental hygienist or an LPN, having other jobs on your resume that prove you have developed certain skills can be a real plus when it comes to landing a job after you get certified.

Jobs like waitressing build multi-tasking and teamwork skills. A busy restaurant requires a certain triage that is perhaps not life and death but certainly can reach crisis proportions like an ER or busy clinic can. Working in restaurants also develops a great feel for teamwork.

Perhaps you spent summers as a lifeguard while getting your bachelor's degree. And to do that you needed to know CPR. Or you were a camp counselor in charge of first aid. These are the kinds of experiences you should keep track of throughout your life and build them into your resume when the skills developed through such work can be applicable.

Even working part time in a veterinary office can teach you skills that are transferable to the human medical world. Medical charts, drawing injectables into syringes, biowaste disposal, and many other details are all the same whether you are working with dogs or people.

Try Different Things

Don't get stuck working part time or volunteering only in the kind of place that you might want to work. Find out what things are like in many different settings. And keep track of the skills you are exposed to in each. If you volunteer in a nursing home even though your ultimate goal is pediatrics, point out on your resume that you learned how to interact with patient's families under stressful conditions.

Getting Hired and
Getting Ahead

PROFILE
Connie Slater
Physical Therapist

Connie Slater became interested in physical therapy in a way that seems common in the health care industry. When she was still in high school, a friend broke his elbow while skiing and went to a physical therapist. His descriptions of what PT involved intrigued her. At the time, teaching and nursing were the main career options for women; to Connie's teenage sensibilities, PT just seemed more cool.

After getting her bachelor's degree (the entry level requirement when she got into PT; entry level now is a doctorate), Connie went to work in a rehab center in the Berkshires in western Massachusetts. There she was exposed to diverse physical therapy work, including helping people recover from strokes, spinal cord injuries, neurological problems, and much else. The center also had outpatient services and a satellite hospital. This gave Connie exposure to different types of treatment and different kinds of facilities.

But she decided maybe teaching was for her after all; a few friends had become teachers and their summers off sounded appealing. Connie left PT and the Berkshires to go to graduate school; but she soon found out that teaching at the college level did not mean summers off. And it meant research, something that didn't appeal to her at all.

So next Connie began working in a pain management clinic, a type of facility common now but unusual at the time. "This is where I got exposed to a holistic approach—the combination of treating mind/body/spirit—that has flavored the rest of my career," Connie says.

From the pain clinic, Connie opened a private practice in the Boston area. She admits it was a daunting task. "You open your doors and pray that people come." But she had developed some unique niches that attracted clients and her practice survived for 18 years.

"One of the reasons I closed was because insurance reimbursement got so low."

She felt she was not able to make an adequate hourly wage given her level of education and amount of experience. Connie closed her clinic and started being a "snowbird"—working in Florida in physical therapy seven months of the year and spending summers in Maine doing whatever job she felt like doing.

"These days physical therapists are in such demand that you can be a traveler, setting up with an agency who will get you long-term temporary assignments all over the country," she explains.

After the snowbird experience, Connie joined a clinic in Maine. "I feel like I have reinvented my career many times, almost starting a new career within the PT field."

And now, full circle, Connie once more has her own practice, Fryeburg Physical Therapy in Fryeburg, Maine. This time she bought an existing practice, meaning she started out with a client base. To have your own practice, Connie explains, "you have to have some business and some marketing skills and interest to make it work." She also advises figuring out if you want your practice to grow or you want to keep it small. Either is fine, but if you want to keep your practice small and don't realize it, things can get out of hand. Or if you want to grow your practice and don't pay attention to that, you won't get where you want to be.

Having your own practice means you can set your hours. But Connie advises finding a location that has a somewhat affluent and reasonably sized population base.

You can still have a great career working in someone else's practice, especially if you go in with a specialty that allows you to have some control over what you do and how you do treatments.

Having just spent several months preparing to hire another therapist for her office, Connie says that the field is experiencing a definite shortage that she doesn't see going away for a while. Some big facilities are even paying for students' schooling ensuring qualified staff two or three years down the road. And the field is headed toward autonomy, without the need for physician's referrals, which will increase the demand even more.

There are a lot of ways to direct your career, Connie explains. But directing it seems to be a key. "A specialty certification is very worthwhile," Connie advises. "I've been in my career a long time; I've seen a lot of trends," she says. "It's a good field and there is great demand."

■　■　■

Once you have the appropriate degree, license, or certification, getting a job in most parts of the health care industry these days is not difficult. As Connie Slater pointed out, some medical professions, like physical therapy, are experiencing a shortage of workers and therefore offer many options to those entering or moving around in that field. However, there a few things to keep in mind.

The Usual Suspects

No matter what industry you're entering, there are standard ways of looking for a job. It helps a lot to use them.

Newspapers

The newspaper classifieds almost always have a separate section specific to health care jobs. Definitely look at these. However, don't consider them the only possible medical jobs in the paper. Look in the regular employment section too, especially if you are looking for a job in health care that could be a more general position—for instance, employers might put ads for medical billing specialists in the medical section, or they might put an ad in the general employment section thinking someone with accounting or bookkeeping experience might be more likely to see it there.

The Sunday papers in major metropolitan areas often have large employment sections, especially health care ads in urban environments with a large number of hospitals.

Job Fairs

Industry-specific job fairs are usually worth the time early in your career, mostly to be able to identify all the possible employers in the area. Bring resumes and hand them out. Dress appropriately for meeting potential employers. It is unlikely you will get a job offer at a job fair, but you might meet the person who will eventually give you your next job. As the old saying goes, you only make a good first impression once.

Informational Interviews

If you have targeted potential employers with whom you think you would like to work, find out if you can meet with them for what is called an "informational interview." This is a no-pressure opportunity to really see if the company is a good match for you. Companies are often open to this, provided the appropriate personnel has time, because the onus is on you not them—they do not have to follow up with letters or phone calls.

Beyond the Same-Old, Same-Old

The same-old, same-old is a perfectly appropriate job searching technique, especially for entry-level jobs. But there are more creative ways to find jobs. And some of these ways are more appropriate and useful after you have been in your career for a while.

Schmoozing

Get to know people. Go to gatherings attended by people in the industry. Call the friend of a friend of your ex-mother-in-law, invite him to lunch, and pick his brain. Personal contacts become the best way to find out about possible jobs once you have established your career and are looking beyond entry-level positions.

The Internet

No longer the big new thing, the internet is quickly becoming the tool to find anything, including jobs. It is also a great way to check out the web site of a medical facility you're considering. You can use the internet to look for educational opportunities in your chosen field.

Some of the medical-specific job sites on the internet include:

- *healthcare.monster.com.* The major job-seeking web site, monster.com, has a health care component that is user-friendly and comprehensive. You can also get career advice, look up articles with tips on things like getting into nursing school or radiation safety, check out a conference calendar, and use its resume center to create, post, and update your resume.
- *www.medicalworkers.com.* Another job search site, it offers e-mail notification of new job postings.
- *www.medjob.com.* This medical job search site has lots of good links to other medical sites.

- *www.medicaljobstreet.com*. Although this seemed like a good site, with the ability to search by state, specialty, or degree type, nothing came up after several searches for nursing positions in the Pacific Northwest or New England, so perhaps this site is out of date. Worth a check back.
- *www.medzilla.com*. This medical job site has great information on its clients (like Merck, Genzyme, Amgen, and others). You can search its client base or by job type. You can post your resume. It also has an interesting salary survey feature where people can post their salaries anonymously. A search of RN came up with a long list, including a registered nurse with 26 years of experience and a BSN degree with a salary of $56,000. The survey did not include regional data, which would explain a lot about salary discrepancies. It also includes links to health care expos, pharmaceutical liaisons, and other medical links.
- *www.hcrecruiters.com*. This site is for an executive recruiter specializing in health care, and has a resume writing function. All fees are paid by the employers.
- *www.careerbuilder.com*. Search under the health care category for jobs. A search of "occupational therapist" in Boston, Massachusetts, came up with four pages of jobs, all posted within the last month.

Advancing Your Career

The first key to moving your health care career forward is to be sure to get some diverse experience when you do your internship, clinical, residency, or whatever on-the-job training you get during your formal education. Then use those experiences to make an informed choice about your first real job in the medical field. The field has a strong enough job market right now that you should be able to hold out for an area in which you are eager to work.

In the Beginning

You may find yourself floundering around a bit for the first year or two, especially if you are in a generalized field like licensed or registered nursing and haven't gone on to specialize.

Maybe you thought second shift would suit your lifestyle, but it's not working out for you. Pediatrics seemed like a good direction for your nursing career, but ultimately you keep thinking back to how much you enjoyed working with the elderly at that nursing home and how much they appreciated you.

What do you do next? Stay there! You don't have to stay in your first job forever, and if it is totally miserable and you are totally miserable with headaches at the end of the day, sleepless nights, and regret about having to go to work in the morning, by all means find something else. But after your first year or two in the field, stop hopping around.

Some things may cause you to have to change jobs sooner than you expected—your spouse is relocated or your mom falls ill and you need to relocate to be closer to them. Life happens, and our jobs are impacted. However, these things can be satisfactorily explained in an interview. Leaving a job after two months just because you don't like it, you find your colleagues hard to get to know, or you don't like the drive is not a good way to advance your career.

Find ways to make the drive more appealing—get some books on tape or find a good restaurant, shopping plaza, park, or a fitness center near work and go there a couple days a week after work to avoid the traffic. Find alternate routes, even if they are longer. A couple months is not a long time to get to know people. Trust that your colleagues will open up after a while. You may be surprised after a year to look back and realize how much you thought you didn't like your job ten months ago but now you do. Things do take time, and you need to be willing to give your job some time.

Once you have been on the job for a year, that experience will really count on your resume. You can barely learn where the bathrooms are and how to run the coffee machine in two months, much less learn any specific nursing or medical-related skills.

You don't want to put job hopping on your resume and you don't want to leave them out and have to explain gaps in your employment history.

What Next?

Two or three years into your entry-level work within your field, you may begin to find that there is an area of specialization that you would like to pursue. Certainly let your supervisor know if something appeals to you; or perhaps your supervisor has already seen that something specific that you are good at and has encouraged you in that area.

If you want to make more money in a specialization, you should investigate getting an advanced degree in that area. And the first thing to check is whether your employer has education benefits that might pay for it. Your company's HR department may have a list of schools that offer degrees in your interest, ones that other employees have used their education benefits to attend.

Be sure there is a market for your specialization, beyond where you are working right now. It may seem like you will be there for a long while, but things can quickly change for reasons over which you have no control.

OJT

On-the-job-training is a great way to advance your skills with no cost to you except for showing up to work. Take advantage of every opportunity that interests you. Many offer certificates that prove completion of a certain type of training.

Advanced Degrees

As Chapters 4, 5, and 6 make clear, many fields offer associate's degree educations that allow entry into a field. From there, you can pursue bachelor's and even master's and doctoral degrees, depending on the field you are in and how far you want to take your specialty.

An advanced degree within a specialty health care field is certainly a way to make more money. But there are two other ways that are probably more useful, especially if a higher salary is your main goal. One way is to get a degree and/or experience in business administration and management. The other is to open your own practice. The latter is covered in Chapter 10.

Find a Mentor

Mentoring in the business world has taken on a formal aspect—including in some cases paying the mentor—in the past ten years. In some businesses, there is no way you will get ahead without a mentor.

On a more casual basis, find someone in your job whose personality and skills you admire and would like to emulate as you develop your career. After you get to know the person better, ask specifically if he or she would consider helping you think through the next stages of your career and make sure you are preparing yourself adequately. When you leave your job, buy your mentor a nice gift as a thank you. Send a new business card as you change jobs to be sure you both keep in touch.

Health Care Management

There are many ways to be a manager in health care. If management is a path you would like to take, you should consider an MBA or other business management degree. Schools like Clarkson College in Omaha, Nebraska, offer programs such as a master's in health care business leadership, a bachelor's in health information management, and other related associate's, bachelor's, and master's degrees. It also has an online component.

Widener University in eastern Pennsylvania has a certificate program in health care management. You need a bachelor's degree to get into this program, but this kind of management certificate is great for those who can't afford the time or money to get a graduate degree.

You can find out about other online management courses in health care at www.online-education-center.org.

Office Manager

An office manager is the person who manages the overall functioning of a health care office—making sure machines are working, keeping supplies stocked, hiring cleaning and repair personnel, and managing those employees who answer the phones, greet patients, and do bookkeeping. This person makes sure the reception desk is always staffed (and probably does it her- or himself if not). An office manager deals with all non-medical-related personnel. (Nurses usually report to the provider, but offices are set up in many ways so that may not be the case in every place.)

Managing People

Managing people can be one of the most rewarding business practices. It is a great feeling to help a loyal employee progress in his or her career. But only you can decide whether managing people is something you are interested in. It is a fine art. You need patience. You need the ability to motivate people. You need to be honest but also protect the best interests of the practice. You need to be able to tolerate listening to employees' woes. And you need to be able to keep enough distance from your employees to reprimand them if the need arises.

Nursing Management

To get into administration in the nursing field, nursing degree candidates should definitely consider a bachelor's degree. Nurse managers often oversee the LPN nursing staff and other RNs. They hire and fire people, assign cases, and set schedules. Nurse managers often don't do much hands-on nursing, but again that depends on the type of environment you are in.

How To Interview

Interviewing in the medical field should not be much different than any other employment interview. Here are six key things to keep in mind for a successful interview:

1. Arrive 10 to 15 minutes early for your interview. More than that is not only unnecessary but too early. Late is completely unacceptable.
2. Dress appropriately for the type of job for which you are applying. If you are applying for an LPN home care

position, you don't need to interview in scrubs and white nursing shoes but a dress and pearls would probably be out of place. Wear business casual clothing that is clean and neat. And be sure your person is neat—check your teeth, check for leftover shaving cream near your ear, that kind of thing.

3. Bring extra resumes, just in case the interviewer can't locate the one you sent or in case other people join the interview. It looks great to be that well prepared.

4. Think ahead of time for some questions to ask of the interviewers. Take notes. Act like an engaged member of the interview. Don't grill them but do give the impression that you are interviewing them as well, that their job is not the only one you have interviewed for.

5. Leave the interview with a definite follow-up plan. Is hiring taking place within the next two weeks? When might you hear next from the company? Know what to expect so you don't need to call and grovel for information.

6. Send a thank-you note. Depending on the type of correspondence you have had with the interviewers, an e-mail may suffice. Most likely you will want to send a short written thank-you note. Keep it simple. And send it the day after your interview—you want it to arrive a couple days later to remind them of you and that they should call and hire you, but not so long that they've forgotten what you look like.

Do plenty of practice interviews. For those jobs you don't get, think how much good rehearsal you are getting for when that perfect job comes along and you want to get the interview just right.

On Your
Own

M.J. Smith's career as a registered dietitian started in a fairly typical manner but has ended up being anything but traditional. With a general interest in the sciences when she started at a small liberal arts college, she eventually transferred to Eastern Illinois University's Clinical Dietitian Program.

During summers while working toward her BS, M.J. worked in the nutrition department in a hospital, doing simple diet instruction and helping select menus for patients on special diets. Always interested in everything about the dietitian field ("I never wanted to just bury myself in one specialty, I was interested in all of it," she says), M.J. found it particularly intriguing to connect the science of dietetics with understanding individual conditions and how they related to food choices and how they could help a person with a real name and real life sitting in front of her at the hospital.

Luckily, the hospital work fulfilled her desire to experience it all. She rotated among pediatrics, cardiology, and many other types of needs, so she got a lot of diversity. "I always loved the hospital setting," she says, "I loved being on a team that helped people feel better."

While doing her required internship after completing her bachelor's degree, M.J. completed her master's. At that point she went into patient education at a major medical center. Her husband was also working at a major medical center, but his goal was to start a rural family practice. When they moved to a small town in Iowa, M.J. found it a real challenge to find her own way to a fulfilling career— there were no major medical centers in rural Iowa.

So she got creative. She began her own subscription service called Menu Management. Each month she mailed a packet of menus, shopping lists, and a newsletter to a 3,600-subscriber base. She hired teenagers to help her stuff packets in the basement. About the same time she was approached by a publishing company interested in acquiring her service, M.J. found herself so busy that one afternoon to appease her young son's need for attention she opened a bag of marshmallow-type treats and gave them to him? Then she thought, "I am giving people from all over the country good nutrition advice and look what I just gave my son." She took the opportunity to sell her subscription service and start thinking of a new way to pursue her dietitian career.

Her small business made M.J. realize that she had the ability to articulate her science. This realization launched a successful writing career that started with her first book in 1990—*All-American Low-Fat Meals-in-Minutes*—which hit the bookstore shelves right when Americans were discovering the meaning of fat grams in their diets. Needless to say, the book was a success.

M.J. went on to write 12 nutrition/cookbooks. "While I was writing," she says, "I was also practicing part time in a small hospital two to three days a week." It was the best of all worlds.

At that point she got weary of the subject and starting writing about other subjects, including a book on the history of the physician, and contributing to other people's books. Recently, she got back into diet-related writing, inspired by her now-college-aged son, Fred. Together they wrote *The Smart Student's Guide to Healthy Living*.

While not the traditional path of a dietitian, M.J. has shown how one can take a health care career and make it as a self-starter. Today, she says, there are more job opportunities than ever for dietitians, especially with an aging population. Independent dietitians tend to be consultants, setting their own hours and working for different agencies. But the three basic settings for dietitians—food service where you are making food, clinical where you are working with patients on a health care team, and community settings like health clubs and weight loss programs—remain the standard employment base.

However, despite the growing need for dietitian care, as with many other segments of health care, the reimbursement climate continues to be a challenge. Not all insurance companies cover such services.

And salaries, while reasonable, may not be quite up to par with stronger salaries in other allied health specialities that have similar requirements in regard to academic rigor (it takes around six years to become an RD).

"But," admits M.J., "like teachers, RDs don't tend to be called to the profession by money. There is something that is so privileged about helping people change their lives. And food is so essential to our lives."

■   ■   ■

M.J. Smith has worked out an interesting and unique health care career. But being on your own in health care typically means having your own practice. Having your practice is nothing more than a different twist on business ownership. Owning/running your own business is not for everyone, but those that are cut out for it can't think of anything better.

However, having your own practice typically means you are at the top of your profession or at the upper levels of the health care field, i.e., a doctor or dentist, not a nurse or dental hygienist. I won't cover that in much detail. There are other ways to be out on your own though; many health care professionals work for themselves as consultants or independent contractors or as floaters working in several different offices over the course of the month.

I'll take a look at ownership first, then at independent contractors because some of the same skills are also necessary here.

Owner Traits

It doesn't matter what industry you are in, there are certain personal traits that will make business success much more likely. Some of these traits include patience, level-headedness, ability to make tough choices, delegation skills, and people skills. Here's why.

Patience

This trait keeps coming up in discussions about health care. Mostly, patience is necessary because much health care involves dealing with the public. When you own your own practice, you will have employees—there's an exercise in patience.

As a business/practice owner, you must also learn to wait for all the pieces to fall into place for your business to even open, much less succeed. Opening a business takes time. Negotiating a lease and hiring staff alone takes time. Be patient. If you map out a realistic business plan, it will incorporate the time it takes to take care of all these details.

Level-Headedness

The owner of a business has to be the one who maintains her or his composure no matter what the circumstances—whether business is slow, fast, or the place is on fire, clients and staff will look to you for how they should be reacting. Learn how to stay calm under pressure in order to make decisions with a clear head.

The other aspect of level-headedness that will come in handy as an owner is to be practical. Don't fall for expensive gadgets and services that crafty salespeople talk you into. Use these traits when interviewing potential employees. A level-headed attitude will serve you well no matter what.

Ability to Make Tough Choices

Being a business owner requires you to be willing to make some tough choices. No business will succeed without a somewhat ruthless owner. You will need to be able to fire employees who are not working out, who are simply not working, who are disruptive to the rest of the staff, who are found stealing from you, or who simply are not valuable employees. You may need to decide to move your practice—despite your love of the building or area you are in. If it isn't conducive to clients, it isn't a good spot for your business.

When business is less than satisfactory, you need to make tough choices to help save money or bring in more clients. When business is great, you still need to be willing to make tough choices in order to keep the bottom line in the black and save money to help when times are not so rosy.

Delegation Skills

This is one of the most difficult things for business owners of any kind. Running a business is a lot of work and in few businesses can you do everything yourself. It is hard to delegate responsibilities for something that is your own personal dream. You know exactly how you want things done—and only you can do things exactly that way. Don't expect your staff to do what you want done in the way you do it. Learn how to let your staff do your thing *their* way. Often how something gets done isn't the key, it's the end result that's important.

Learning to delegate is very hard but worthwhile. As you interact with your employees, think about whether you are delegating or not. If things aren't getting done the way you would like, make sure you are clearly communicating what your final goal is. Ask your employees for their input—and make sure they believe you really care about their input by carefully considering it and putting good ideas into action.

People Skills
There is barely a job on earth that doesn't require some level of people skills. Owning a medical practice ranks way up there—you need to have good people skills for your employees and for your clients. The fact that your clients are probably coming to you not under the best circumstances makes people skills that much more crucial. Learn how to listen. Make sure you take what people say seriously and don't dismiss their anecdotal evidence just because that is not your experience. Learn to be kind and confident; it is a good mix for a business owner.

Buying vs. Start-Up
You can start from scratch with your own practice or you can buy an existing practice. It will depend on what is available for sale in your area, how fast you want to get up and running, and also your experience, personal resources, and situation.

Buying an Existing Practice
Medical professionals sell practices all the time—they burn out, they retire, they find that their side interest of selling antiques on eBay is more rewarding. You can find a practice for sale by contacting a business broker. Or you can put the

word out to people you know in the field—tell your own dentist you are interested in buying a dental practice, or your chiropractor, or your nurse practitioner.

You can also talk with people at business gatherings like the chamber of commerce social events and conferences. Word of mouth really can be the best way to get into a practice.

Are you working for a practice already? Any chance it might be for sale in the near future? You won't want to outright ask—this is basically admitting you are going to be leaving your job—but you might put a couple feelers out there.

Start-Up

If you want to get into your own practice fast, start-up is probably not the route to take. Finding the right space, negotiating a lease or a purchase, designing the layout, ordering and installing equipment, hiring people to staff the business, and developing clientele can easily take more than a year.

Business Plan

No matter what route you are taking to get out on your own, you will want to have a business plan. The more complicated your venture, the more complex your business plan will be. Business plans are critical for getting loans and other financial assistance to buy your business or get it started, and they are also a good road map to follow and constantly refer back to as your business develops.

The basic elements of a business plan include

- a synopsis of your business idea,
- market analysis of competitors and other factors figuring into the potential success of that industry/field in the area in which you plan to conduct business,
- a marketing plan, detailing how you plan to reach potential clients,
- a financial plan, showing how you will finance your business purchase or start-up, as well as operating expenses for at least one year (three would be better),
- your experience, and
- the experience of any staff you have coming on board.

Nothing says you need to follow every detail of your business plan—you can veer off the plan as you go along. But without a plan to start with, you aren't veering off, you are simply winging it.

Other Ways of Being On Your Own

There are other ways to be in health care and be on your own. As you see in the profile at the beginning of this chapter, writing books, articles, and other education materials is one way. Other jobs in health care lend themselves to self-employment, such as a medical illustrator.

The way that many people work on their own is as a consultant. Of course, it takes many years for you to gain enough experience in your field to be hired as a consultant and have enough clients to be a financial success.

The floater approach, where you work for several different practices, can give you more independence than the traditional work-in-one-office approach. Some floaters actually work full time for an agency that gets the work for them (and takes a share of the profits, of course).

The health care field today is just bursting with opportunities for the entrepreneurial type to make a new path to success.

Resources

Web Sites

American Medical Association (www.ama-assn.org)

American Occupational Therapy Association
  (www.aota.org)

American Physical Therapy Association (www.apta.org)

Healthcare Careers (www.health-care-careers.org)

Health Care Hiring (www.healthcarehiring.com)

Health Care Jobs (www.healthcarejobs.org)

HealthQuist (www.healthquist.com)

National Council of State Boards of Nursing (www.ncsbn.org)

U.S. Department of Labor, Bureau of Labor Statistics
(www.bls.gov)

Books

Bennett, Scott. *The Elements of Resume Style.* AMACOM,
2005.

Blitzer, Roy J. *Hire Me, Inc.—Interviews.* Entrepreneur Press,
2006.

Damp, Dennis V. *Health Care Job Explosion.* Bookhaven Press,
2006.

Lesonsky, Rieva. *Start Your Own Business, Third Edition.*
Entrepreneur Press, 2004.

Marino, Kim. *Resumes for the Health Care Professional, 2nd
Edition.* John Wiley & Sons, 2000.

Glossary

Anesthesiology. The science of using certain chemicals/gases to make patients unconscious for medical procedures.

Associate's degree. A post-secondary degree that typically requires two years of college-level classes.

Bachelor's degree. A post-secondary degree that typically requires four years of college-level classes.

Cancer. The uncontrolled reproduction of invasive cells within the body, usually within an organ.

Cardiology. Referring to the heart/circulatory system.

Client. A term used to refer to people who see medical practitioners.

Clinic. A place where medical treatments are done.

Clinical. On-the-job training done by someone still in school, usually required to complete a degree.

Complementary medicine. Using both Eastern (acupuncture, massage, homeopathy) and Western medical practices (surgery, drugs) to treat a patient.

Critical care. Caring for patients with life-threatening diseases/injuries.

Doctorate. A post-graduate degree beyond the bachelor's, considered a terminal degree, i.e., there is no further education in the field.

Geriatrics. A branch of medicine that deals with diseases and conditions related to aging.

Gerontology. The study of aging.

Home care. A growing part of the health care field, in which medical care is done within the home.

LPN. Licensed Practical Nurse.

LVN. Licensed Vocational Nurse (used in Texas and California instead of LPN).

Master's. A post-graduate degree that typically takes two years beyond a bachelor's. Has become the entry-level requirement for some fields.

Nephrology. Referring to the kidneys.

Nurse practitioner. A registered nurse who has completed a doctorate and can, in some states, open an independent practice as a primary caregiver.

Otorhinolaryngology. Referring to the ear/nose/throat.

Outpatient. A patient who is not admitted to spend the night in a medical facility.

Palliative care. Treatment designed to make a patient comfortable, particularly in terminal illnesses where treatment is no longer viable.

Patient. A term used to refer to people who see medical practitioners.

Pediatrics. The care of children, typically newborn to 18 years.

Radiology. Refers to the field in which one works with x-rays.

Rehabilitation. The restoration of a sick or injured person by therapeutic means.

Scintigraphy. A branch of nuclear medicine where a radioactive compound is introduced and then tracked in the body by a scanning mechanism that produces an x-ray-like image.

Telehealth. Providing care and medical advice through electronic media such as teleconferencing or over the internet via web sites and chat rooms.

Therapy. Various means by which practitioners help people restore health.

Index